DECORATIVE ARTS
of the Amish of Lancaster County

Daniel and Kathryn McCauley

DECORATIVE ARTS
of the Amish of Lancaster County

Daniel and Kathryn McCauley

Good Books

Intercourse, Pennsylvania 17534

Acknowledgments

Catherine H. Anthony; Judi Boisson: New York, Westport, Southampton; Lars Cain, Manassas, Va.; Esprit Quilt Collection, San Francisco; The Free Library of Philadelphia, Rare Book Department; Ivan Glick; Barbara S. Janos; Smith and Wanda Johnson; Anne and Bob Klemeyer; Landis Valley Museum, Lancaster, Pa.; Jay and Susen Leary; Maureen and Gregory McCauley; McCauley Law Offices; Muddy Creek Farm Library; The People's Place, Intercourse, Pa.; Paul and Lorraine Wenrich; Tom and Anne Wentzel; Eve and David Wheatcroft.

Design by Craig N. Heisey

Photography by Jonathan Charles, except: pp. 19, 106 and 118, Joan Broderick, courtesy of The Free Library of Philadelphia, Rare Book Department; pp. 46, 48, 61 and 72, courtesy of Esprit Quilt Collection, San Francisco; pp. 49 and 52, courtesy of Barbara S. Janos; and p. 88, courtesy of Smith and Wanda Johnson Antiques.

Decorative Arts of the Amish of Lancaster County
© 1988 by Good Books, Intercourse, PA 17534
International Standard Book Number (hardcover): 0-934672-66-0
International Standard Book Number (paperback): 0-934672-69-5
Library of Congress Catalog Card Number: 88-81264

Library of Congress Cataloging-in-Publication Data

McCauley, Daniel.
Decorative arts of the Amish of Lancaster County.

Bibliography: p.
Includes index.
1. Decorative arts, Amish.   2. Decorative arts—
Pennsylvania—Lancaster County—History—19th century.
3. Decorative arts—Pennsylvania—Lancaster County—
History—20th century.   I. McCauley, Kathryn.   II. Title.
NK835.P4M38   1988   745'.088287   88-81264
ISBN 0-934672-66-0
ISBN 0-934672-69-5 (pbk.)

For our children, Dan,
and Cayce,
and for R.G. Klemeyer
who supported our
endeavors from the start.

Preface

We found, in researching this work, that very little definitive information on the decorative aspects of Amish material culture has been published. It made documentation difficult; consequently much of the information we present here is a synthesis of a decade of contact with the Amish, as well as Pennsylvania German cultural historians, antique dealers and collectors. We believe all our findings are accurate and supported by facts as presently interpreted. We hope our work will stimulate additional interest and investigation and will increase the pool of knowledge, as well as correct any errors we may have inadvertently included.

A multitude of people have supported us and contributed important opinions and pieces of information to this work. At the risk of omitting any of our sources, we want to thank the staffs of The Free Library of Philadelphia, Philadelphia, PA; The Heritage Center of Lancaster County, Lancaster, PA; The Lancaster Mennonite Historical Society Library, Lancaster, PA; The Library of the University of Pennsylvania, Philadelphia, PA; The Landis Valley Museum, Landis Valley, PA; The People's Place, Intercourse, PA; The Pequea Bruderschaft, Gordonville, PA; and the Pequea Publishers, Gordonville, PA.

Abner Beiler, Joe Beiler, Amos Fisher, Amos Hoover, Aaron Glick, Ivan Glick, Ephraim Riehl and Levi Stoltzfus helped us with Amish history. Amos Hoover of the Muddy Creek Historical Library, Denver, PA, and Lois Huffines of the Department of Modern Languages, Bucknell University, Lewisburg, PA, gave us assistance with translations.

For insights into Amish decorative arts, their history and how the products relate to and reflect their culture, we consulted with Annie Beiler, Ike Beiler, John Ebersol, the Flaud family, the Fisher sisters, Mary Hostetler, Arie Lapp, Steve Scott, David Riehl, David Wheatcroft, Francis Woods, and the many Amish families who invited us into their homes, sharing with us their heirlooms and the history and the folklore surrounding them. Finally we wish to thank all the collectors who have shared both their treasures and knowledge with us.

—*Daniel J. and Kathryn M. McCauley*

The Amish and
Their Decorative Culture

Alphabet Sampler
Rebecca (Lapp) Smoker, 1885
16 ³/₄ × 18 ³/₄
Wool yarn on Berlin canvas
Private collection

Berlin canvas gradually replaced both whole cloth and punched cardboard as a foundation for samplers during the last quarter of the 19th century. Canvas was widely accepted because the open mesh fabric facilitated the counting of stitches. Available at stores throughout the community and by mail order, it was easy for rural women to obtain.

It is customary for Amish samplers to display several alphabets. Here there are three: a small format for marking linen, a German style probably copied from one of the printed German alphabets circulating in the community at the time, and a large, capital, block-letter alphabet distinguished by a floral bloom in each of the letters.

This latter style became very popular with Lancaster Amish women after 1880. Its origin is uncertain, but it was widely adopted for marking garments, particularly women's shawls. The large, brightly colored letters aided in the quick identification of one's property at church or other gatherings. In a society where most garments look the same, this small innovation proved exceedingly popular. Variations of this alphabet continue to be used today for this very reason.

Rebecca Lapp was born August 18, 1873, the sixth and last child of Michael K. and Rebecca Lantz Lapp. Becky married Samuel P. Smoker on October 18, 1892. They had seven children before Rebecca became ill and died prematurely at 31 years of age, January 15, 1905.

The material culture of a society is composed of its tools, clothing, architecture and decorative arts. It is a physical expression of the commonly held beliefs and philosophy of its members. In a traditional society the old pass the mores, motifs, symbols, beliefs and values to their young, who in turn repeat the process. A group commonality of mind begets a commonality of expression which is passed from generation to generation. Each generation in turn edits the material culture to reflect its own values and experiences.

Amish decorative arts are an embodiment of the Amish culture: they exhibit the lifestyle of that distinct, religious community and the personality of its inhabitants. Although the Amish are a living and growing community today, *Decorative Arts of the Amish of Lancaster County* will examine the work these people made during a particularly distinctive period— 1860–1940.

The traditional nature of the Amish who lived in eastern Pennsylvania from the middle of the 19th century to the mid-20th century is exemplified by their adherence to traditional Pennsylvania German art crafts like the sampler and fraktur. Their lifestyle as country farmers is projected in the utilitarian nature of their artifacts. The community's commitment to the "plain" life is projected through the astounding simplicity and "clean" form in the design of their creative work. The ideal of community itself is personified in the profusion of shared patterns in their artistic products.

At the same time, the personality and individuality of each maker comes through in color choices and modifications of designs. In fact, many products sharing the same pattern are startlingly different. For example, Lancaster Amish alphabet samplers reveal significant color and format variations, all on the theme of the alphabet.

Sociologists and cultural anthropologists agree that the products of a people may provide a medium through which to discover their interpretation of life and their relationship to it. Thus, it is possible for us to see the Amish through a window of their own making—their decorative arts and crafts.

Who Are The Amish?

For over two hundred fifty years the Amish have been a presence in Lancaster County. They came to colonial Pennsylvania from Germany, the Alsace and Switzerland in the early 1700s. (Settlements later developed throughout the Midwest and Canada.) As Anabaptists they trace their beginnings to the 16th century, when the idea of voluntary adult baptism first emerged. This was a theological understanding in direct conflict with then accepted European religious thought. Consequently, these people were persecuted for their radical beliefs and many chose to seek a more tolerant religious climate in the New World.

The Amish are a Christian group who believe the Bible to be the literal Word of God. From their inception they have professed that pride and self-willfulness cause disharmony, not only among people, but also between humankind and God. They view these as primary hindrances for each person to overcome with the help of God and the church. As a result, they place a high value on humility and try to foster it in every aspect of life.

The Amish today and in the past have followed a doctrine of nonconformity to worldly ways. They exist "in" the world but attempt not to be "of" it. This is a result of their literal interpretation of passages in the Bible, such as II Corinthians 6:7 which states: "Wherefore come out from among them, and be ye separate, saith the Lord."

Separation from the world has taken many forms among the Old Order Amish. One visible sign has been their dress code. Fashionable clothing is deemed worldly and prideful, so plain dress, with many variations from community to community, has been a part of the discipline. The men, in general, wear their hair cut square across their foreheads and long enough to cover their ears, and after marriage grow beards without mustaches. All wear dark broadfall trousers held up by suspenders. Their hats are distinctive—usually flat, broad-brimmed, and of black felt or straw. Their vests and jackets usually close with hooks and eyes, rather than buttons.

Old Order Amish women wear long dresses of unpatterned material in such colors as maroon, navy, purple or dark green. Adult women's dresses have no buttons but are fastened instead with straight pins or snap fasteners. Aprons and kerchief-like shoulder capes cover the dresses for modesty's sake. An Amish woman keeps her hair long, coiling it into a tight bun, and covers her head with a white covering. When going away, women wear black bonnets. In cold weather they wear wool shawls, often with jackets or coats underneath.

Plain dress serves as an outward expression of these people's faith and a visible sign of their unity. It symbolizes the boundary between the Amish and non-Amish and dramatizes their commitment to separation from the world.

The Old Order Amish continue to use horses and buggies for transportation and horse-drawn implements for field and farm work. That, too, is a conscious choice. Automobiles are not viewed as inherently evil, but are seen as a threat to family and community life. The Amish believe that the auto provides easy mobility and so could disrupt the social fabric of their community. Deep social and communal relationships are a major goal. The congregation, composed of neighbors and friends, is the intended focal point of the Amish world. The horse, as transportation, is a self-imposed aid to help attain this objective. It limits social contacts to distances easily reachable within a reasonable amount of time by buggy.

Renting the services of a van or bus, or utilizing the train to travel to a distant settlement, is permitted, but the ownership of a car is seen as being more threat than blessing and is thus rejected.

Trends, fads and rapid modernization are considered signs of worldliness. In order to reduce the influence of the outside world and the intrusion of so called "progress" upon their lives, the Amish have consciously controlled the pace at which they accept change. They revere tradition and do not readily discard it. The Amish do not necessarily view technology as evil, in and of itself, but they are concerned about its potential impact upon their society.

For example, to date the Amish of Lancaster County have rejected the use of electrical power produced by public utilities. Diesel generated electricity, required to keep bulk milk tanks cool on dairy farms, is allowed, but the use of commercially generated power is forbidden. Amish leaders feel that allowing unlimited use of electricity would usher in the acceptance of a host of luxuries. It could undermine the discipline of the people

Bunch of Grapes Drawing
Fannie Beiler, 1908
5 1/8 × 7 3/4
Hand-drawn and colored on laid paper
McCauley Law Offices

Fannie L. Beiler was a niece of Henry Lapp, the daughter of his sister Fannie who married Jacob Beiler. Obviously influenced by Henry, young Fannie L. did a series of drawings between the years 1907 to 1912. Representative of these pieces, this work mirrors Henry's in both color and subject.

Animal, vegetable, floral and fruit paintings from Fannie L.'s hand have been documented. While her palette is consistent with that of other Amish artists, favoring deep saturated colors positioned against bright greens and blues, Fannie used the same freedom of expression in the selection of color for her subjects as Henry did for his.

Graphic impact as opposed to realism was her goal. Orange grapes, blue apples and other unusual hues are commonly found in her work, resulting in surprising renditions of otherwise mundane subjects.

and stretch the fabric of the society.

For example, the Amish kitchen is amply yet modestly outfitted to service large farm families. But the adoption of electricity would likely mean the advent of convenient appliances, thus changing the pace of these people's lives and undermining the time-honored practice of having generations work at basic tasks together. Once such a large gate to innovation is opened many fear it would be very difficult to control and impossible to close. The leaders feel that it is safer and easier to leave such a door closed.

Community Life Is Cultivated

While the Amish world may appear unbending and colorless from the outside, it is actually quite the opposite. Members hold family and interpersonal relationships in high esteem. Community life is fostered through frequent visits to relatives and friends.

The very structure of the church is designed to further a feeling of community and belonging. Congregations are small, each consisting of about 30 families, a number that can comfortably be accommodated in a home for Sunday services. Each congregation is led by a bishop, two ministers and a deacon, who are selected by lot from the group. Every other week the congregation gathers in a house of a different member to worship and socialize. Responsibility for the poor, sick or grieving is shared by the congregation. From birth till death members are surrounded by a support group that will go to great ends to assure that their physical, emotional, psychological and religious needs are satisfied.

Farming is the vocation of choice for the Old Order people, primarily because it is a family endeavor. All contribute, allowing everyone to be together at home. The Amish family literally eats, sleeps, works, worships and plays together. All members have a place and value. Children are received as gifts from God, parents are respected for accepting the responsibility of a family, and grandparents are especially valued for their knowledge and experience. From birth to death, close family relationships are nurtured.

Large families are considered a blessing since many hands are needed to run a labor intensive farm operation. Children are given chores, thereby easing the work load for the adults, while at the same time instilling a sense of responsibility and discipline in the young. They learn, from the time they begin to walk, that work is a cardinal moral tenet in Amish life.

On most Amish farms the parents retire in their late 40s or early 50s and move into smaller quarters known as the *gross dawdi haus*, an apartment attached to the main house. Farming responsibilities are surrendered to one of the children (usually a son) who is in the midst of his child-rearing years.

It is a rewarding system for all concerned. Young mothers have ready access to wisdom and support since an older woman's years of parental experience are always at hand. The young farmer, meanwhile, has close at hand the advice and help of a man with thirty or forty years of experience. Furthermore, the elderly are encouraged to continue to participate in farm work which provides them with a sense of purpose and self worth. The gross dawdi haus becomes the center of activity for the young children who receive care and attention from both parents and grandparents.

Diamond in the Square
Unattributed, circa 1935–1945
84×84
Wool and crepe
Catherine H. Anthony

Diamond in the Square or Center Diamond quilts were known as "Halstuch" to many of the Amish. This is a reference to the triangles bordering the diamond that resemble the *halstuch* or shoulder cape worn by Amish women over their dresses.

A fully developed example of the diamond pattern, this piece has corner squares on the outer, inner and diamond borders. Variations of this pattern range from this colorful and active design to simple, yet sophisticated, two-shape geometrics.

Here the deep maroon center is offset by a shocking pink border with small corner squares repeating the center color, a subtle device that helps control the contrast. A similar effect is obtained by repeating the green of the triangles in the corner squares of the second pink inner border. The purple outer border is highlighted by large green squares and a pink binding.

As is typical of Diamond quilts, the center is star-quilted and the wide border is decorated with feathers.

A sense of sharing is pervasive among these people. The Amish adhere to the ideal that they are their brothers' keepers, and express this value through mutual aid. Their concept of community requires that they care for one another, as manifested by the deacon who collects alms twice a year and supervises the administration of these funds to needy members.

The Amish do not accept unemployment or welfare payments from the government but choose to support those members who require assistance. An example of the depth of their commitment to mutual aid can be seen at the time of a death. As word circulates that a person has died the women from the congregation begin to arrive at the home of the bereaved and take charge of the household chores. Friends and relatives are welcomed and made comfortable. Lodging is arranged if necessary. Meals are cooked and children cared for. At the same time, men from the congregation take over the duties on the farm and prepare the grave. The grieving family is relieved of all responsibility. A surviving widow's fields are worked and crops gathered by men from the neighborhood.

In times of crisis the Old Order feel compelled to offer support not only to members, but to outsiders who are in need. Frequently, when natural disasters such as tornadoes occur, Amish volunteers hurry to the scene to assist in the clean-up and rebuilding, volunteering not only their time, but often materials as well.

Gatherings such as barn-raisings and quilting bees are another kind of community event. Called "frolics" by the Amish, the name reveals their attitude toward such affairs. Although these are work days, socializing is a by-product. These events have often stimulated Amish material decorative culture. Quilt, rug and other patterns are often discussed, and creative ideas shared and refined.

Simplicity Held in High Regard

Today, as in the past, Lancaster County Amish homes reflect the people's commitment to a simple life. Walls are painted white or light green and are devoid of decoration, save for a few functional items like calendars, family records or perhaps a shelf clock. The windows may have shades, usually green, but curtains are prohibited. In the past the floors have been polished wood, but linoleum is becoming popular. Homemade rag rugs are acceptable, but wall to wall carpet is seldom used. Furnishings are simple. There are comparatively few upholstered chairs and sofas. Seating around the table at meals is on benches or plank seat chairs.

The Amish ideal of simplicity has fostered a lifestyle in which persons aspire to happiness through self-fulfillment, family and friends. The gathering of material goods is seen as an act of pride and is to be avoided. Art, at least in the decorative sense, is viewed with skepticism. Drawings and paintings are rare. When they are encountered they are often modest in both size and composition to conform as closely as possible to the precepts of simplicity and austerity. The artwork that does exist has usually been made as keepsakes or remembrances for close friends or family.

The restraint and plainness of the Old Order way of life has presented an opportunity for the evolution of a unique decorative material culture. The cycle of farm life provided the spare time required for craft production. The relative isolation of the Amish and their limited outside contact retarded the pollution of their art by extra-cultural influences. Conse-

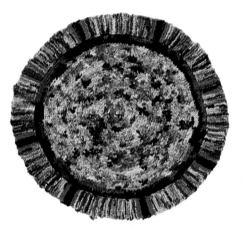

Braided Rug, crocheted edge
Mary (Lapp) Lantz, circa 1890–1910
34 inches in diameter
Cotton
Private collection

Worn-out garments are the usual source of material for "rag" rugs and carpets. As a result, almost all Amish rugs are dark. This example, however, has a predominance of light shades. The crocheted edge is separated from the braided center by a dark loop of braiding which defines a border between the crocheted and braided work. The multi-colored crocheted edge is organized by eight black and red dividers spaced evenly around the perimeter.

Another unusual feature of this rug is its shape. Most Lancaster County Old Order braided rugs are oval, rather than round.

13

quently, their choice of patterns has reflected their basic and serious view of life. In addition, their separation from the world allowed them to ignore convention and experiment with colors and motifs of their own.

The Amish skepticism toward art did not result in rejecting beauty, but led instead to its refinement and simplification. The result has been the evolution of a decorative material culture that is neither over-designed nor austere, but one which reflects what these people saw: the harmony of nature and the creatures that inhabit it.

The Development of Amish Decorative Art

The decorative art of a group or community is both the individual expression of its makers and a material synthesis of the culture itself. Social scientists have postulated that when a new idea or image is presented to a group it is not necessarily accepted or rejected. It is broken down to its essence and compared to the traditional standards of the group. If the new image is found to be of value, it is usually integrated into the older format and a composite results that reflects the attitudes and needs of the group.[1] Thus, as ideas and environment change, so does the material and decorative culture.

Like most subcultures, the Amish did not evolve in a vacuum. Their neighbors exposed them to ideas and art forms. These ideas were evaluated and those found appealing were adopted and modified to reflect Amish attitudes, values, culture and perceptions of life. Like many societies, the Lancaster Amish were borrowers. The quilt, which became one of their most noted art forms, was borrowed from their English neighbors. The Amish modified it to reflect their culture by creating unique patterns, uses of color and quilting motifs.

As Lancaster County Old Order society germinated, evolved and blossomed, so did a distinct decorative culture. Its development can be divided into three distinct stages: the early (1720–1850), the middle (1850–1940), and the late, or modern stage (post-1940). The art products, usually crafts, of the early period reflect the common cultural heritage shared by the Amish and other Pennsylvania German immigrant groups. Although they had diffuse religious orientations, they all originated in the same region of Europe. Consequently, the products of one group are visually similar to those of the others. They brought their material culture to the New World and ingrained it into their children, It took several generations for this influence to diminish. Thus, early Amish works are frequently indiscernible from those of related Germanic groups, such as the Mennonites.

However, between 1850 and 1870 the Amish in Lancaster County began to display an identifiable decorative art of their own. Unique adaptations of traditional crafts and motifs, particularly in regard to pattern and color, began to appear. It is during this period that we see the appearance of the distinctly Amish color palette. What is now recognized as an "Amish look" began to emerge in their samplers, door towels, quilts, fraktur and other art crafts. The development of this unique material identity parallels the maturation of the society as well. A number of important events coincided to induce the crystallization of this new material culture.

Prior to 1850 the Amish community was too small to have the self-reliance and independence necessary for the establishment of a clearly unique

Rag Doll
Unattributed, circa 1880
Cotton; rag stuffing
The People's Place

This doll is important because its original wardrobe documents late 19th century Amish clothing. The dress lacks the vertical double-breast pleat seen on post-1900 dolls, yet has the decorative cuff and hem pleats. This suggests that the breast decoration evolved later. The bonnet has the high crown seen in Lancaster today, but it also has the elongated neck flap shortened about 1910. The petticoat is red calico with a green applied border above the hem—an implication that undergarments were more colorful during the 19th century.

The doll's body is similar to pieces made 80 years later. This shows how the Amish pass ideas and traditions from generation to generation.

14

cultural identity. It was not until 1843 that the first congregation grew large enough to divide in two. However, after this initial division the church prospered. By 1860–1870 the population had grown large enough to more effectively resist outside influence. As the Amish began to provide more goods and services for each other, these products took on a more distinctive "Amish look."

During this period the Civil War erupted. Governmental and public pressure was exerted upon the Amish to induce them to support the conflict. Their tenet of nonviolence, a basic principle of the church, required that the faithful not participate in the war. The situation served to isolate the Amish and prompt unity among them. It contributed to the development of stronger communal ties, which fostered the formation of a stronger cultural identity.[2]

The Industrial Revolution was, by this time, beginning to bring prosperity to agrarian America and the Amish. Labor-saving inventions like the harvesting machine, treadle sewing machine and factory-loomed textiles helped provide the time necessary to produce the artifacts that remain today as examples of this distinctive, decorative material culture.

At the same time, the cash generated by improved productivity allowed the Amish to avail themselves of store-bought cloth, brightly dyed thread and yarn. Among the Lancaster Amish, cheap, readily available, colorfast cloth and thread were quickly adopted and became mediums with which to express a developing decorative consciousness.

Another ingredient in the development of an independent Amish material culture was the church division of 1877. A split that moved along "conservative" and "liberal" lines, it separated the marginal members from the committed. The result was the strengthening of the bonds among those who chose to remain Old Order. The committed stayed, the church was strengthened, and an enhanced cultural identity resulted. All these events served to promote the evolution of the communal identity necessary to produce a uniquely Lancaster County Amish material culture, exemplified by the diamond quilts they began to produce about this time.

Essential to any appreciation of Amish decoration is an understanding of their concept of pride. For the Amish, pride is *the* cardinal sin. They constantly attempt to balance humility and simplicity against vanity. Consequently, the arts produced by the Amish manifest their attempt to maintain this balance. Beauty tempered with simplicity is the result.

While the rejection of pride and worldliness laid the groundwork for unusual results, another factor contributed substantially to the flavoring of their decorative material culture: their suspicion of "art" in the popular sense. The *Ordnung*, the code of conduct that governs nearly every aspect of Amish life, outlines how members should express themselves. Art for art's sake was unacceptable. It was not only perceived as worldly, but as a waste of time as well.

But by the mid-19th century, the ministry found it necessary to make certain concessions in defining acceptable decor.[3] Flower gardens, since they were organizations of nature's beauty, were allowed. Amish women to this day favor colorful gardens to brighten their yards. When subtle artistic changes crept in that were deemed nonthreatening, the ministry may have frequently opted to look the other way rather than risk initiating a controversy. Consequently, evolution in artistic design was slow.

Doll Quilt: Sunshine and Shadow
Unattributed, circa 1950–1960
19 1/4 × 19 1/4
Wool, cotton
Private collection

Made from dark dress scraps and hand quilted, this piece has the look and appeal of pre-1940 Amish design. It was probably made in the mid-1950s by a grandmother for her granddaughters to use in the doll crib. In quality, design and construction, it mirrors a full-size piece, even to the exaggerated tape binding. This piece shows how some women, particularly the older generation, continued to produce pieces that reflect traditional roots, even after most of the Amish community had developed a taste for lighter shades and synthetic fabrics.

Door Towel
K B (Katie Beiler), circa 1910
17 × 45 ¼
Cotton thread embroidery on linen
Private collection

This hand-done embroidery stitching illustrates a style adopted by the Lancaster County Amish women about the turn of the century. Cross-stitch was, by the early 1900s, considered somewhat old-fashioned in Amish circles. Like most later towels this one is profusely decorated. By this time, exhibiting proficiency in needlework through embroidering on towels and quilts was less likely to be thought worldly.

Katie Beiler made this towel shortly before she was married, probably between 1910 and 1915. She decorated it from top to bottom, as was commonly done during this period. (These towels were made by Amish women as late as 1948.[4])

The upper border of Katie's towel is drawn thread work, accomplished by removing strands of the horizontal weave. The lower section is an applied hand-needled lace made in the "bunch of grapes" pattern. Grapes were a popular design motif with the Amish after the 1880s and were a common quilting design. Katie applied a knotted fringe to the bottom of her towel.

The more creative persons in the Amish community likely experimented first with decorating utilitarian objects or designing new rug or sampler patterns. If the church leaders did not censure the maker of the object, a new design was born. This slow process was one of the reasons the Amish appear to adopt an art form so much later than their neighbors.

Usually they did not broadly adopt an art form until it was no longer fashionable among other Pennsylvania German cultures. A survey of the popularity of folk crafts in the non-Amish community reinforces this finding. For example, while samplers and fraktur were most popular among the Pennsylvania Germans between 1790 and 1820, they reached their height of acceptance in the Lancaster Amish community probably between 1870 and 1910. This phenomenon appears to extend so universally across Amish crafts as to be a rule of thumb: the zenith of a traditional craft within that religious community was approximately 50 years later than it peaked in other, more mainstream groups.

The ethic of hard work is projected into crafts made by the Amish. They have believed that any job worth doing must be done well without any effort spared to accomplish this end. The result is a decorative material culture that reflects careful design selection and attention to detail. One can see the results of this attitude in the prolific and meticulous quilting evident in almost any quilt made in Lancaster County prior to 1940. It is also manifest in the shading of hues in floral hooked rugs and the careful cross-stitching on decorated pillow covers. Amish work consistently demonstrated patient hands rendering well composed and detailed art work.

Features of Amish Decorative Arts

Natural themes permeate Old Order Amish material culture. Family record samplers are often decorated with floral vine borders and may have butterflies or birds as motifs. Pansies, forget-me-nots and other flowers dominate many hooked rugs. Furniture is often enhanced by a simple painted wood grain decoration. Even most fraktur bookplates bear floral decoration. Rejection of "worldly" opulence is reflected by the choice of natural designs which foster the values of simplicity and humility, the essence of Amish living.

The Amish palette is composed of the natural colors that are part of their world. The darker basic colors they have selected for their dress are the basis of their textile arts. Their traditional aversion to pastel shades seems to reflect their identification with nature and the land they work.

In the 19th century household linens were so valued that initials or inventory numbers were stitched onto blankets, pillow shams, bolster covers and other textiles. Over time in the Amish community, this initializing took on a form of embellishment, and surviving examples indicate that by the second half of the 19th century bed dressings became the subject of profuse decorative embroidery. Often names, dates, flowers and a myriad of other motifs were carefully hand embroidered on linens meant to be included in the dowry of both the bride and groom.

The popularization of loomed rag carpets during the 19th century increased Amish interest in coverings for their polished wooden floors.[5] When, by 1860, loomed carpets were permitted by the church, they were of plain colors and without the stripes that were fashionable in other Pennsylvania German communities.[6] Small braided and hooked rugs also gained favor. In fact, the hooked rugs became canvases upon which women could fashion small floral and occasionally animal scenes.[7] These rugs added a splash of color to stark rooms and became an extremely common vehicle for artistic expression.

As Amish farmers became more prosperous and furniture more affordable, blanket boxes, wall cupboards, chests of drawers, desks and other pieces of furniture found their way into Amish homes. Much of this furniture was made of inexpensive softwoods. It was often decorated with paint to enhance it and give it the look of a richer wood.

The advent by the mid-19th century of readily available, relatively inexpensive china and glass brought these goods to the attention of the Amish, who gradually began to collect them.[8] Small pieces of china, souvenirs of trips to Canada, Indiana, Ohio and other settlements, began to appear in Amish homes. Cup and saucer sets, embellished with gold-leafed "Mom" and "Dad," were popular throughout the country at the time and found favor with the Amish. Pressed glass bowls and pitchers were given as gifts and, as a result, collections began to form. Corner cupboards became commonplace in Amish parlors to house these treasures. Today the corner cupboard is a ubiquitous fixture throughout Lancaster County in which the women display collections of glass they have gathered or inherited.

The profusely and ornately painted furniture commonly recognized as having a Pennsylvania German origin was not a product of the Amish.[9] Instead, as a rule, Amish furniture tended to be simple in design, functional and constructed with a keen attention to detail that resulted in a product of high quality.

For reasons of simplicity and humility, the use of printed or patterned fabrics in dress was not permitted.[10] The taboo against printed fabric in Amish clothing had a significant effect on their textile art, particularly their quilts. Because they did not use patterned fabrics for shading and contrast they were forced to accomplish that dimension solely through the manipulation of color. The result has been a quilt and textile art form marked by the use of daring contrasts of color that often render a strikingly graphic effect.

The proscription against wall decoration of almost any kind, including wall paper, also affected Amish decorative material culture. Drawings and paintings are rare since they were understood to serve no practical function and so could not be hung. Hooked rugs and quilts, on the other hand, were produced in great numbers since they could be used and displayed.

Among the Amish, academic or formal training in the arts was simply not considered a possibility. Those who engaged in drawing or painting appear to have been completely self-taught. Their lack of academic instruction is evidenced in work which tends to be flat in its dimension. However, this has served to preserve a naive quality that in the best sense represents the Amish as a people.

The sanctions against photographs, sketched or painted portraits and other graven images, which were increasingly enforced by the ministry during the 1860s, had a profound effect upon their art.[11] Human images are extremely rare and when encountered tend to have minimal facial detail.

The mid-twentieth century marks the end of the age of originality of design for the Amish. The pollution of their society by the intrusion of

Boys Shirt
Unattributed, circa 1840–1860
21 inches long, 16 ½ inch waist, 9 inch sleeve
Cotton
Private collection

White linen or cotton pullover shirts were worn by Amish men from the 18th century through the 19th. Colored shirts became progressively more popular as cheap, colorfast fabrics became available during the second half of the 1800s. Today white shirts are all but reserved for church and "dressy" occasions. The pullover seen here has been replaced by a button-front style. Still mostly homemade, the modern shirts lack the decorative gathering around the collar and shoulders seen here.

extra-cultural influences became too strong. Amish society, like many American subcultures, felt the drive of "progress" and the modern industrial age. Land pressure drove up farm prices, and cash became more important than ever. Tourists generated a demand for souvenirs and the Amish answered with the quilt, one of their traditional cultural products which they began to produce in unprecedented numbers. The result has had two significant effects on their material culture. First, quilts are now made to the virtual exclusion of the other traditional Amish crafts, and second, the dark Amish colors and traditional designs have been supplanted by the pastels, printed fabrics and patterns that appeal to outsiders.

The best of Lancaster County's Amish material culture remains those pieces made by Amish men and women to decorate their homes in ways that conformed to the precepts of their church and society. These items were personal expressions valued by both maker and family. Yet, the truest value of Amish decorative culture is its testimony regarding the Amish people. It projects their strength and vibrance. It traces their cultural evolution. But most of all it captures the beauty of simplicity.

Roots of the Amish Church

The Amish trace their origins to the Protestant Reformation that swept central Europe during the 1500s. As reformative ideology evolved, the idea of infant baptism came into question. Some people began to believe that the concept of sin required an understanding that children did not have. They also believed that commitment to a religious philosophy was a serious matter requiring the knowledge and experience that comes with maturity. Therefore, infant baptism, the outward sign of such a commitment, was viewed as meaningless. Persons who developed this conviction came to be known as "Anabaptists," meaning "rebaptizers."

In Zurich, Switzerland on January 21, 1525, a group of adults baptized each other as a sign of their voluntary commitment to faith, and a radical Anabaptist movement was born. The step was seen as an affront to the government and state church alike, since it signalled a move toward separating church and state. Branded as heretics, the Anabaptists were subjected to wide persecution and the eventual martyrdom of almost four thousand people.

The movement flourished despite persecution and quickly spread into Germany, France and the Netherlands. In February, 1527, the basic guidelines for a faithful church were agreed upon at a ministers' conference held at Schleitheim on the Swiss-German border. Known as the "Schleitheim Articles," these tenets enumerated seven major themes that are still the foundation of Amish church discipline. Basically, they addressed adult baptism; the ban, or shunning, as a disciplinary action; communion as an expression of fellowship; separation from the secular world; the duties of the ministry; refusal to participate in the government and rejection of militarism; and the detriment of oath-taking. [12]

In the Netherlands, Menno Simons, a Catholic priest, began to question the Church's position on infant baptism and the consecration of the host during mass. In 1536 he turned to Anabaptism and, being a prolific writer, organizer and administrator, eventually became an important Dutch leader in the Anabaptist movement. Those who joined him became known as

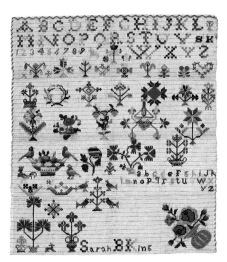

Alphabet Sampler
Sarah B. King, 1890–1895
20 ½ × 25
Wool yarn on Berlin canvas
Private collection

Quite large for an Amish sampler, this piece allowed Sarah to include two alphabets and over forty decorative motifs. Almost every variation of the "pot-of-flowers" theme is represented. An exceptionally extensive collection of large designs is also present. While for the most part traditional, the sampler includes some modern motifs, such as the pot of roses at lower right. This pattern became a favorite for needlepoint pincushions during the early 20th century.

When Sarah crafted her sampler, decoration that was more representational, less stylized, was gaining favor among the Amish. This change in taste made traditional Pennsylvania German sampler motifs, and to some degree the sampler itself, archaic.

Daniel Zook married Sarah in 1906. They went on to have nine children. As a result of the school crisis in the late 1930s, they moved to Maryland along with several of their married children. [13]

"Mennists" or "Mennonites," the nickname eventually given to the far-flung group.

In 1632 another significant ministers' meeting was held at the Flemish Mennonite Church in Dordrecht. The result of this gathering was a document of eighteen articles that represented the Anabaptist confession of faith. For the first time a "creed" was formulated and circulated. Printed in Dutch, German and French it became extremely popular. Known as the Dordrecht Confession, it remains central to Amish belief today. [14]

Jacob Amman was a Swiss-born leader in the Alsatian Anabaptist community. This Anabaptist group was more cautious than their Dutch sisters and brothers in using shunning as a form of discipline for the membership. Amman, however, was strongly influenced by the philosophy of Menno Simons who advocated shunning, or the *Meidung*.

A leader concerned with the vitality and purity of the Church, Amman, during the summer of 1693, proposed that communion be increased from once to twice a year. He also advocated that excommunicated members be disciplined by shunning, that the church adopt the Dutch practice of feet-washing as taught in the New Testament and that the membership evidence a rejection of worldliness through distinctive, modest dress. His proposals found favor with many but resistance from others, causing a rift in the leadership. Those who chose to follow the more conservative principles of Jacob Amman became known as "Ammonites," or Amish. Philosophically, they had more in common with the Dutch Mennonites than with their Swiss brethren. The writings of Menno Simons became a cornerstone for the Amish ministry and remain so to this day.

A Move to America

Adopting a philosophy that was at odds with both the state and the state-approved church brought the Anabaptists oppression and persecution. Government-sponsored purges forced them to abandon the city for a more hidden rural existence. Farming became, and for the Amish still is, their vocation of choice.

State-sanctioned persecution plagued the Amish and other Anabaptist groups in Europe for over 100 years. In the early 18th century, land sales agents for Pennsylvania, a religiously tolerant colony in the New World, circulated throughout central Europe promoting colonization. Determining that this was an opportunity to escape oppression, some Amish undertook the hazardous journey to the English colony. They began to arrive in Philadelphia before 1725. [15] A major migration took place between 1737 and 1800, during which time about 500 Amish arrived in America. [16]

The fervor of these people for religious freedom was manifested by the hardship they endured to establish themselves in the New World. The cost, in terms of time, money and lives lost, was high. To get from central Europe to the American colonies during this period often took a year of travel. One began by selling one's possessions in an attempt to raise the fare. Often these funds were exhausted by the time the family paid the travel, lodging costs and tolls required to get from Switzerland to Rotterdam. Numerous customs houses existed along the Rhine at the time, each adding to the expense and delay. [17]

The next step, the voyage across the Atlantic, was made on commercial vessels specializing in this trade. The passages were overbooked and over-

Flowers Drawing
Unattributed, dated 1811
Hand-drawn, lettered and colored on
laid paper
Free Library of Philadelphia

This drawing, while simple in overall composition, has a well designed flower and bud design that is typical of Amish attention to detail. The German script on either side of the flower is the date—"in the year of our Lord 1811"—manifesting the strong religious orientation of its creator. In the mound below the flower are the words, "This belongs to Anna Stoltzfus."

Anna (1799-1870) was probably the second child of John and Veronica (King) Stoltzfus. She would have been about 12 years old when she either executed this piece or was presented with it. She married Christian Petersheim, an Amish immigrant, about 1820. They lived on a farm in Mascot, Lancaster County, and had five children. Anna died August 18, 1870, at the age of 70 years, 8 months, and 21 days. It is from this obituary date that her birth date, November 27, 1799, is calculated.

Bookplate
Barbara Ebersol, 1871
4 5/16 × 7 9/16
Waterpaint on lined paper
Private collection

Barbara Ebersol was a prolific bookplate artist who marked as many as several hundred books for her people between 1860 and 1920. Many of her works were done on lined notebook paper. She probably drew the plates in a notebook, then cut them out and glued them into the inside cover of the book. As a rule her format was to paint a motif slightly below the center, then hand-letter the owner's name above it, along with the date on which she did the work. She usually bordered her plates with a barber-pole or leaf-vine pattern, although she did occasionally use others.

For bookplates Barbara seems to have favored floral motifs to the geometric and sampler-like themes she sometimes chose. The tulip is, for her, a rare design. She appears to have made her first tulip plate in red and orange colors in 1863. The more refined design shown here is one of several similar tulips to have been discovered, all dated in the 1870s.

Barbara marked this book for Susan King who was born October 4, 1852 and married the Amish watchmaker Abraham Beiler in the mid-1870s. The book descended through the Beiler family.

crowded. Diseases like scurvy, dysentery and seasickness were rampant and took scores of lives. Virtually no passenger under the age of seven survived the crossing. The hardships were extreme. Arguments, fights, stealing, cheating and similar antisocial behavior between passengers and family members were common. [18]

By the time the ship arrived the funds of the passengers were often depleted. Consequently, family members often sold themselves into servitude for periods as long as seven or eight years to pay the balance of the passage debt. Even if one managed to pay for the passage, upon debarkation one was often short the amount required to purchase a land grant. So men were usually forced to work for wages while attempting to save the sum necessary to buy a farm.

The year 1737 is a milestone in American Amish history. On October 8th the ship "Charming Nancy" sailed into Philadelphia from Rotterdam. [19] Amish colonists from this ship founded two settlements from which seventy-five percent of all present-day communities have developed. [20]

The larger of the two colonies was the "Northkill," founded by nineteen Amishmen from the "Charming Nancy." They located along the ridge of the Blue Mountains between the Schuylkill and Susquehana Rivers, approximately eight miles north of Reading, Pennsylvania. Although now Berks County, this area was in Lancaster County at the time and was opened for colonization in 1732, shortly before the Amish arrived. The land was inexpensive and attracted many Amish settlers. The Northkill suffered from Indian raids in the 1750s and, although the settlement survived, discord gradually developed and the church began to disintegrate. Most of the Amish families moved out by 1800 and the settlement dispersed. [21]

The first permanent settlement is believed to have been started by passengers from the "Nancy" who moved into Lancaster County along the Conestoga Creek, an area presently known to the Amish in the area as the Upper Mill Creek. Seven individuals believed to be Amish moved into the Conestoga area. Although the records are cloudy, it appears that Johannes Gerber was the first Amishman to locate there. He was probably followed by Christian Smucker, Jacob Kurtz and Jacob Schantz (Johns). [22]

The initial settlers in this area were scattered, as opposed to the Northkill where most of the immigrants located. Although a very early church is believed to have existed and worship services held, the colony was only marginally established before 1750. [23]

The Amish bishop David Beiler, writing in 1862, referred to this as the first Amish church in America: the "West" or "Old" Conestoga Church. [24] The settlement stretched from Eden, along the current Route 23, to Hinkletown, along the current Route 322, south of the Welsh Mountains. [25] As the colony prospered, worldly influence asserted itself and the members became lax in their discipline. After 1775 church membership steadily declined, until by 1800 it almost ceased to exist.

At this time Christian Stoltzfus, who had left the area in 1770, was ordained bishop and again took up residence along the Mill Creek. A man of strong faith and commitment, he is credited by historians with restoring the values of the church and saving the colony. [26]

Four other colonies were formed in Lancaster County: the Cocalico, the Compass, the Conestoga Valley and the Pequea. It is undetermined if any Amish settled in the Cocalico area prior to 1737, but the church was more than likely established by 1742 and lasted until about 1800. Some of the Amish families residing in this area during this time were Blanks, Fishers, Detweilers, Hertzlers and Millers.[27]

The Compass church district extended from the present village of Spring Garden, along the present Route 340, to the Chester County border. Initially colonized by the Dr. Hans Blank family as early as 1760, the population moved in from other settlements so that growth did not result from immigration from Europe. At first the congregation was under Bishop Jacob Mast of the Conestoga Valley. Toward the end of the century Peter Blank became a bishop and took responsibility for the settlement. Some of the early family names associated with this church were Kurtz, Zook, Gerber, Wanner, Sauder, Hooley, Sommers, Reichenbach and Troyer. Over time the congregation gradually became lax in its discipline and by the 19th century it dissolved.[28]

The Conestoga Valley church (Morgantown) was founded in 1760 by Bishop Jacob Mast who moved down from the Northkill. Located in the Churchtown area this settlement survives to this day. Some of the founders of this community were Christian Beiler, Christian Hertzler and John Yoder.[29]

The Pequea settlement, from which the larger Lancaster County Amish community descends, began in 1790 when Jacob Zook moved from the Conestoga settlement to a farm near Gordonville. In the next twenty-five years Amish people from at least five different settlements in eastern Pennsylvania established themselves in the Pequea community. These are the ancestors of the present King, Beiler, Stoltzfus, Lapp and Fisher families which are the most numerous surnames in the present Lancaster Amish community. The northern part of this settlement was known as the Millcreek area and may have been somewhat separate from Pequea from the beginning but did not become an independent church district until 1843.

The inability of many early Amish settlements to endure resulted from a number of factors. The communities were small and scattered. They usually consisted primarily of family groups and relatives. Consequently, family ties were stronger than church influence.[30] When a member drifted the entire family often followed.

Because the membership of the early Amish church was very small, the members were forced to depend on their neighbors for many goods and services. This outside contact allowed marginal followers an opportunity to be influenced by their more "worldly" neighbors. The small population also meant that some members looked outside the faith community for spouses. More than likely, this influenced some to abandon their conservative ways.

As the Amish became more prosperous fewer children chose to join the church. Current research indicates that less than forty percent of the children of early Amish immigrants chose to adopt the faith or raise a family in the Amish church.[31]

The Amish did not proselytize, so their numbers did not increase substantially by adding converts from beyond their community. At the same time, they became the target of evangelical groups like the Dunkards and United Brethren. It was not uncommon for entire families to be enticed away from the Amish church by the more evangelical groups. The Dunkards were particularly effective in wooing Amish converts. During this time

Doll Cradle
Unattributed, circa 1900–1920
8 × 17 3/4 × 10 3/4
Pine
Private collection

This cradle was made from scraps of an old pine crate. Across the bottom is printed, "do not place close to boilers," a warning that once protected the contents.

The cradle is cut in a pattern commonly used for full-size examples throughout southeastern Pennsylvania during the 18th and 19th centuries. Large round terminals blunt the ends of the rockers to keep the cradle from tipping.

Wall Cupboard
Henry Lapp, 1902
53 × 83 × 21 ¾
Walnut, poplar
The People's Place

Several Dutch cupboards like this one signed by Henry Lapp and dated 1902 are known. Their construction is nearly identical. All have full-pane glass upper doors and blind bottom ones. Henry added blocks in the door corners to give the upper glass and bottom panels an oval shape.

The upper and lower interiors in all known cabinets are painted robin's-egg blue. Each side at the opening between the two candle drawers has a scalloped corner block, which appears to be a purely Lancaster County Amish design feature, and is possibly an innovation of Henry's. The upper and lower outer edges are chamfered with lamb's-tongue termination, common on Lapp's cabinetry.

Overall, the piece has a Victorian look that appears to have dominated Amish taste after 1850.

both groups dressed conservatively, spoke the same language and were located in close proximity. The Dunkards had an orientation and an assertiveness that strongly attracted the Amish, and quite a few converted.[32]

The Revolutionary War also adversely affected the Amish church. The heavy influx of German immigrants into an English colony sparked governmental concern. A Declaration of Allegiance to the crown was instituted in 1727 to be signed by all non-English speaking immigrants as they disembarked. During the Revolution this oath caused a dilemma for the Amish. Their faith required that they respect the government and thus honor the pledge which they had to sign; it also required that they remain neutral and non-militant. Many Amish refused to support the rebellion because of its violence, and so were branded Tories. Several were jailed.[33] Conversely, some Amish youngsters supported the Revolution and decided to participate. It is believed that a number were killed in action.[34]

A decision to support the war was a rejection of the basic Amish principle of nonviolence. It probably caused controversy and division within the church, resulting in a loss of membership. Research indicates that severe population loss occurred during and after the Revolution.[35] It is interesting that almost all the early settlements—Old Conestoga, Compass, Cocalico and the Northkill—peaked just prior to the Revolution, strongly indicating a causal relationship between church membership and the impending war.

The old Conestoga settlement illustrates the leakage of members in the early church. The recently discovered Alms Book, a charity record kept and passed from deacon to deacon, reveals that Abraham Kurtz was an early deacon. Christian Schowalder is believed to have been the minister, and probably the bishop.[36] Both of their names and the surnames of Holly, Johns, Reichenbach and others have been identified as Amish but have long ceased to be family names in the Amish Church in Lancaster County.

Since the Amish hold bi-weekly Sunday worship services in the homes of members, the size of a congregation is dictated by the number of people that can comfortably be accommodated in a house. The average congregation consists of about thirty families. When it grows too large, a church is divided and two groups are formed.

In 1800 only two of the original Lancaster County Amish communities remained with any substantial stability: the Conestoga Valley and the Millcreek Pequea. The attrition of members had so retarded growth that it was 1843 before one of these congregations divided. This occurred in the Millcreek church, which separated into the Pequea and Millcreek churches under Bishops David Beiler and Johannes Stoltzfus.[37] By the time of the Great Division in 1877–1878, there were six established congregations in Lancaster. Today there are over ninety Old Order Amish congregations in the Lancaster County area.

The Amish Church in Lancaster County During the 19th Century

Bishop David Beiler, writing in 1862, described the Amish of an earlier time. He related that their homes were sparsely and simply furnished. Sofas, desks, bureaus and rag carpets were not found, and possibly not allowed. Wooden shoes were common. Wagons were not painted. Harnesses, bridles and saddles were unadorned. Clothing was simple and homemade. The bright colors the Amish adopted, as store-bought cloth became economical, were not allowed in the early church.[38] Bluing was not used and ironing was not done. Shutters and window shades were not permitted. Bishop Beiler lamented that by the mid-19th century many of these things had changed and "worldly" influences were exerting themselves in the churches.

The 1860–1880 period saw the Amish in Lancaster County survive an upheaval that tested the church's roots. A rift started in the more liberal Amish groups in Indiana in the 1850s and spread eastward. It reached the more conservative congregations in Lancaster County about 1870. Centered along liberal versus conservative themes, the main issues involved changes in customs such as adopting the use of meetinghouses, a controversial mode of baptism in which water was poured on the heads of applicants as they knelt in a stream, a less comprehensive use of shunning and less restrictive dress codes.[39]

Several factors contributed to the breadth of the controversy among the Amish. The church had spread geographically west to Iowa and north to Canada, making it difficult to maintain commonality in customs and practices. Different interpretations of the Ordnung, or church doctrine and practices, began to evolve. Furthermore, the years 1815 through 1860 saw a new migration of Amish from Europe. These Amish had a different history and evolutional experience than their American brothers and sisters and tended to be more liberal. Most of these new arrivals settled in the Midwest and Canada, contributing to the development of more liberal philosophies in these areas.[40]

Thus two distinct camps were emerging during the mid-nineteenth century. The basic differences centered on the Ordnung and how it should be regarded. One faction felt it was meant to evolve and change with the times and needs of the church; the more conservative group considered the Ordnung an enduring code of conduct that should undergo alteration only after serious consideration and careful planning. Not only were the questions of meetinghouses and dress causing friction, but so were responses to the Civil War, involvement in political activity and acceptance of innovations such as lightning rods, photographs, insurance and lotteries.[41]

To address these and other questions, ministers from across the country met annually between 1862 and 1878. The goal was to attempt to reach a common understanding on the issues confronting the church. The more conservative members were particularly concerned with preserving simplicity and retarding the encroachment of worldly influence on the church community. By the time the first meeting was held in Ohio in 1862 the conservatives had lost their enthusiasm for the project. The liberal faction had promoted the meetings, organizing and controlling their agendas. By 1865 a philosophical division had, in effect, taken place. As a result, fewer conservative ministers attended the meetings each year.[42] All that remained to occur was for a formal and physical split to take place.

The major issue in Lancaster County was whether the church there could continue to have relations with the more liberal groups throughout the country. The conservative ministers in Lancaster County, under the leadership of the senior bishop, David Beiler, called for a severing of relationships. This caused considerable consternation among the congregations,

Table
Unattributed, circa 1840–1880
16½ × 20½ × 27⅞
Pine, walnut drawer face
Private collection

Small tables, similar to the one pictured here, served as sewing stands or as end tables, positioned next to chairs and beds to hold coal oil lamps. The turnings on the legs, yellow painted drawer, white porcelain pull and overall proportions are typical of Amish pieces, particularly several documented as the work of Henry Lapp. On the back of the drawer is a pencil inscription, "Lizzie F. Beiler, 1870."

Lizzie was born May 29, 1860, and died October 17, 1884. The table passed to her brother David, who in turn passed it to his daughter Lizzie. If the table was actually made in 1870, is was made prior to Henry Lapp's entrance into the cabinet business. It appears likely that at least some of Lapp's patterns were acquired from another craftsman, probably the man Lapp apprenticed under, whose identity remains unclear.

many of whose members had family and friends in these communities.[43] The controversy festered and became so severe that communion could not be held in the Pequea district for several years. Finally, in 1877, the Pequea group divided into an Old Order congregation which continued to meet in homes, and a more liberal Amish Mennonite group which soon began to hold their services in a meetinghouse. The church building was opened in 1882 and the name, "Millwood Amish Mennonite Church," adopted. The "Amish" designation was dropped in 1955.

A similar division occurred in the Conestoga district, resulting in the formation of the Conestoga Amish Mennonite Church. In many instances the separation moved along family lines. As a result, the names of Mast, Umble, Kennel, Summers, Kurtz, Newhauser and others were lost to the Old Order Amish in Lancaster County. The severity of the division is attested to by the fact that the Conestoga Valley church was so weakened that it was fifty-four years before this group was again large enough to divide into two congregations.[44] Although later splits occurred in the Old Order Amish church in Lancaster County, none was as serious in terms of membership loss.

The 1877 division was not without its positive aspects. Actually, it strengthened the Lancaster Old Order Amish church. Those who chose to remain were committed to its values, and the growth of the church has continued steadily. Only two confrontations have resulted in a split since then. In 1890 the Old Order Amish minister Moses Hartz was placed under the ban by his fellow ministers for a variety of reasons. He left the Old Order and began to affiliate with the more liberal Conestoga Amish Mennonite Church. When the Amish Mennonites received Hartz into their fellowship, that act became the catalyst for polarizing the two groups, who had already been in tension. Active relationships ceased. In 1909, an Old Order group who disapproved of the stand taken by their ministry appealed to the Amish church in Mifflin County for ministerial mediation. John Zook and Samuel Peachy responded. A settlement could not be reached and thirty-five families withdrew from the Old Order church. These families formed a new church, which changed little philosophically from an Old Order posture over the next twenty years, except to soften the use of the ban. They did not put people under the ban for joining another church within the Anabaptist family, but they did use it in other ways or for other offenses.[45]

John A. Stoltzfus, who was ordained bishop of the group on April 26, 1926, was very progressive and moved the church in a liberal direction, eventually allowing automobiles and Sunday School.[46] A second split resulted, with the more conservative members remaining with their current minister, Christian King, and the liberals following John Stoltzfus, who aligned his church with that of Moses Beachy from Somerset County. In 1930, these two more liberal groups began to exchange ministers. In time, Stoltzfus and Beachy were asked to assist other groups with change. Since Beachy involved himself more often in such matters, the term "Beachy Amish" began to evolve. In Lancaster County the group continues to be known as the "John A. Stoltzfus" or "Weavertown" Amish Church.

In 1966, the last notable split occurred in Lancaster. David A. Miller, an Old Order preacher from Oklahoma, spoke in Lancaster in 1952. It is said that his philosophy was controversial and appealed to quite a few people, particularly the younger members. When Miller returned home he was

Knife Box
Unattributed, circa 1840
Decoration possibly Barbara Ebersol,
circa 1860
12 1/4 × 5 1/4 d × 7 5/8 h
Poplar, painted red, overpainted mustard
Kathryn and Dan McCauley

Lift-top boxes were commonly used on Pennsylvania German farms to store candles, knives, spices, sewing notions and other household items. This example was owned by Simon (1819–1886) and Barbara (King) Zook (1824–1917), who were neighbors to the Ebersol family. According to family tradition, the box was decorated by Barbara Ebersol when the original red finish began to show wear. It is painted in the colors Ebersol favored early in her career.

Upon Barbara Zook's death, the box passed to her namesake granddaughter (born 1877), who inscribed her name in pencil inside the lid. The younger Barbara never married. She used her box to store a collection of spoons inherited from grandmothers and aunts. When Barbara's possessions were divided, the box was passed to a niece from whom it was purchased.

greeted by a letter from the ministers of the Lancaster churches, severing relations with him and his congregation. But the movement he initiated in Lancaster, while quiet, remained unchecked. In 1966, it surfaced when thirty-five families from the Morgantown area left the Old Order and formed a New Order Amish congregation. Since a minister accompanied the group, it was viewed as a split within the church and the Old Order ministers did not invoke the ban. This group has subsequently divided several times and ranges in practice from the use of horse-drawn carriages and the maintenance of Old Order dress to those who use meetinghouses and allow cars. [47]

Today the Old Order Amish church in Lancaster County is a vital, growing group whose membership has nearly doubled in the last twenty years. In contrast to some earlier times, at least eighty percent of the young people choose to join the Old Order Amish church. Furthermore, there has been little migration out of Lancaster County by the Amish in the last decade, again a change from the '60s and '70s when many families moved to other states and less heavily populated areas of Pennsylvania.

Paint-Decorated Cigar Box
Leah Lapp, circa 1930
_9 ¼ × 2 ⅝ × 5 ⅝_
Paint over soft wood
Private collection

Leah Lapp paint-decorated objects for friends and relatives for a quarter of a century. She seemed to most enjoy painting small boxes and tins, and often presented them as gifts. This piece is one of a pair of common commercial wooden cigar boxes Leah decorated and gave to her friend Barbara Ebersol about 1930. The owner used them to store a collection of small silk handkerchiefs. The Amish used to present such small tokens as handkerchiefs to each other as keepsakes.

Leah was partial to blue-green or bright red as the ground color for her work. Red floral motifs, particularly roses or petunias, dominated her design. The goldfinches (distelfinks) were one of her favored decorative subjects. Her straight-line border tended to be thin and understated.

While Leah commonly added the initials of her recipient and a commemorative date, she seemed to have been reluctant to use full names. Nor did she sign her works or put presentations of any kind inside the lid.

Although known to have done paint-decoration as early as 1928 and as late as 1955, Leah was most active from 1930 through the mid-1940s.

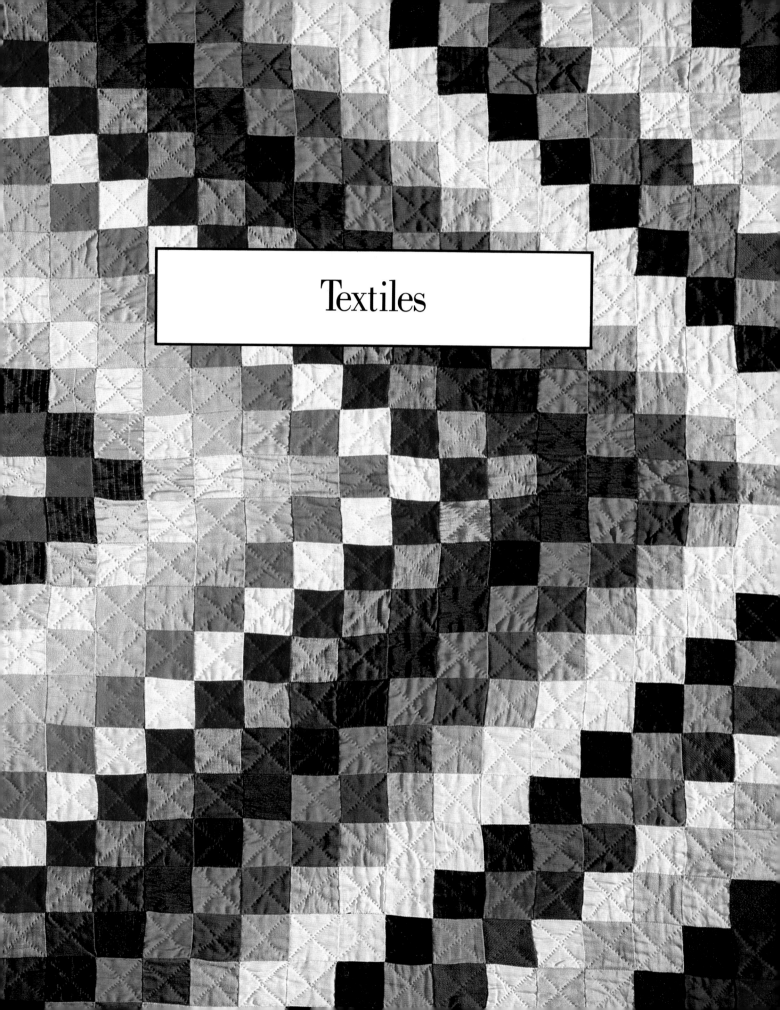

Textiles

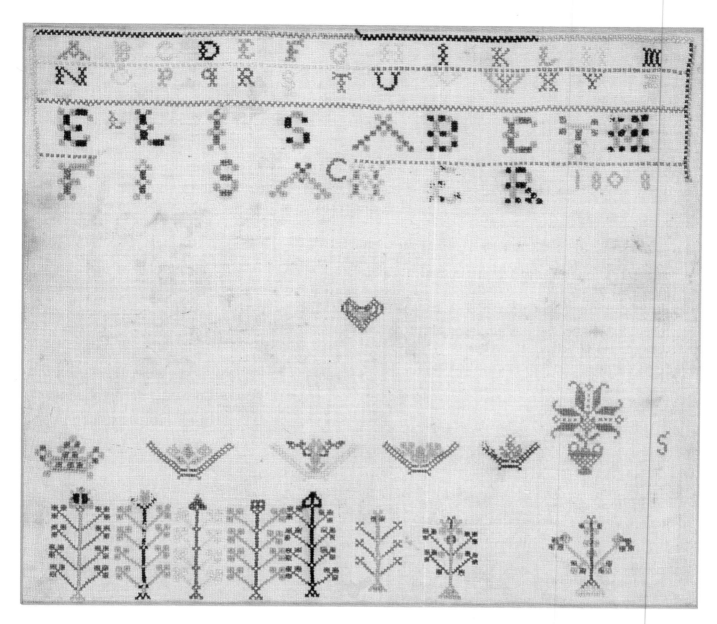

Alphabet Sampler
Elizabeth Fisher, 1808
9 ½ × 10 ½
Cotton thread on homespun linen
Private collection

Elizabeth Fisher's sampler exemplifies the simplicity and beauty of Amish culture. Her alphabet and name are contained in the upper band of activity; decorative tree motifs appear in the lower band. The middle field is open, save for a small central heart.

Elizabeth was born January 19, 1791. She was the sixth child of Bishop Christian Fisher (1757–1838), a leader in the early church.

About 1809, Elizabeth married David Beiler, Sr., who became one of the most influential conservative Amish leaders. Her sons Christian and David Jr. also became prominent leaders. Daughter Catherine was a minister's wife, and Elizabeth's youngest child, Benjamin, was a fraktur artist, some of whose work is included in this book. The most well known conservative family in Lancaster, the Beilers were related to the most well known liberal family by the marriage of David Jr. to Maria Stoltzfus, daughter of "Tennessee" John Stoltzfus.

Amish needlework pictures are rare, and this piece is particularly noteworthy. A young Amish girl's aspirations for a traditional red-brick farmhouse of her own, brightened by a colorful flower garden, are idealized by the artist. The distelfinks (goldfinches) are a personal touch. Lydia fancied these birds and throughout her life put seeds out to attract them. She finished her picture by filling the sky with a yellow moon between two stars. The entire theme is organized within a unique tulip border.

Lydia Smoker was born January 8, 1893. She completed this picture when she was twenty, the year before she married Josiah Beiler. Lydia is known to have created a number of needleworks during her lifetime. She was influenced by her namesake grandmother, Lydia Zook, who produced a needlework from which young Lydia copied the stars presented here.

Lydia felt it inappropriate to display this very decorative piece on the first floor. It hung in the more private quarters upstairs until her death, when her possessions were divided among the family. Considered old-fashioned by modern Amish standards, it was rescued from the attic of one of Lydia's descendants.

Needlework Picture
L.S. (Lydia Smoker), 1913
17 ¾ × 17 ¾ (including frame)
Wool yarn on Berlin canvas,
original oak frame
Kathryn and Dan McCauley

Alphabet Sampler
Sarah Konig (King)
Silk thread on homespun linen, silk binding
Kathryn and Daniel McCauley

Alphabet samplers served a functional, rather than decorative, purpose
for Pennsylvania German women, providing templates from which initials,
numerals and decorative motifs were copied onto family linen.[1] They were
usually stored in chests or drawers until needed and not framed or hung.[2]

Sarah King's sampler, typical of very early Amish work, is similar in color,
material and design to pieces by non-Amish Pennsylvania Germans of the
period. One of the earliest Lancaster Amish samplers to yet surface, this piece
attests to the existence of a shared, artistic heritage, binding the Amish in
Lancaster County to their neighboring Pennsylvania German groups.

This sampler includes two alphabets, Sarah's complete name and over
eighty traditional Pennsylvania German design motifs. The small alphabet
was a pattern for marking bed and other domestic linen. The large letters and
designs were more often applied to door towels.

Sarah was born about 1804 to Solomon and Veronica (Schmucker) King
in Berks County, Pa. Shortly after her birth, Solomon moved the family to
Lancaster County, where this sampler was made. After Solomon's death,
Veronica moved the family to Mifflin County, where she married Bishop
"Long" Christian Zook.

Sarah married Joseph Zook, and after his death, Solomon Yoder. She
appears to have spent her entire married life in Mifflin County.

G H I K L M N O P Q R S T U V W
O N I G H M M I A R I 1818 D E N
D E F G H I K L M N

Alphabet Sampler
Lydia H. Beiler, 1865
12 ¼ × 16 ¾
Wool yarn on Berlin canvas
Kathryn and Dan McCauley

Lydia H. Beiler was born about 1834 to Jacob (1809–1855) and Nancy (Hertzler) Beiler (1814–1844). Lydia made this alphabet sampler, dated 1865, at the unusually mature age of thirty. Surviving examples indicate that Amish samplers, like those made by other Pennsylvania German sects, were usually made by teenage girls between the ages of 12 and 17.

Like most samplers made after 1850, this piece has fewer and larger motifs than are usually encountered on early works. While most of the decoration is very traditional, an unusual, contemporized flower appears in the center of the bottom row. This sampler shows the transition in taste taking place in the Lancaster Old Order community during the 1850–70 period.

Since they were not made for decoration, Pennsylvania German samplers were not always carefully balanced or organized.[3] However, Susan Esh took particular care in the composition of hers. The alphabet is evenly spaced and carefully positioned above a field of twenty-three well designed and located motifs, below which is her name. She enclosed her work in a floral-chain border highlighted with blooming floral-stem corners. The bright red and pink she chose to dominate her piece came into favor among her people after 1850.

Susan's sampler demonstrates the change in the look of Amish handcrafts after the mid-19th century. It has a clearly Amish presence in design and its contrast of bold, hot colors against soothing greens and purples.

Susan was the firstborn child of Jacob and Sarah (Lapp) Esh, arriving December 19, 1880. She married Levi Z. Fisher in December of 1901, after which they took up residence in Paradise, Lancaster County. They had five children. Susan died in 1963 at the age of eighty-two, three years after Levi.

Alphabet Sampler
Susan Esh, circa 1890
12 × 14
Wool yarn on Berlin canvas
Private collection

Memorial Sampler
Susan Fisher, 1887
18 1/4 × 22 1/2 (including frame)
Wool yarn on punched cardboard,
original frame
Private collection

Family records and memorial samplers were two of the very few items allowed to be hung in Amish homes. Usually found in the parlor, a room frequently used for weekend visitors and opened for church services, they were available for all to see. A concession to decoration, they are a testimony to the value the Amish place on family and genealogy.

Two customs of the Amish are illustrated here: the recording of the age of the deceased, including the number of days, and the rendering of a memorial verse. Both are still common practices. The Victorian custom of retaining a lock of hair was also popular and can be seen here at the bottom, where the initials "RK" for Rebecca Kauffman are positioned along with a braid of her hair.

The sampler was executed by Susanna (Kauffman) Fisher to mourn her brother Samuel and her two sisters, Salome and Rebecca. Named for her mother, Susie (King) Kauffman, Susanna married John Fisher in 1879. They were childless.

Her sister Rebecca, born in 1863, was relatively younger than Susanna, who, as is the Amish custom, probably took a very active role in raising her. Farm women busy with housework, their vegetable gardens and large families, depended on older children, particularly daughters, to help raise their younger siblings. A special affection may have existed between Rebecca and Susanna. Rebecca's death moved Susanna so deeply she expressed her grief by making a memorial. Her choice of a morning glory vine to organize her work is an interesting play on words.

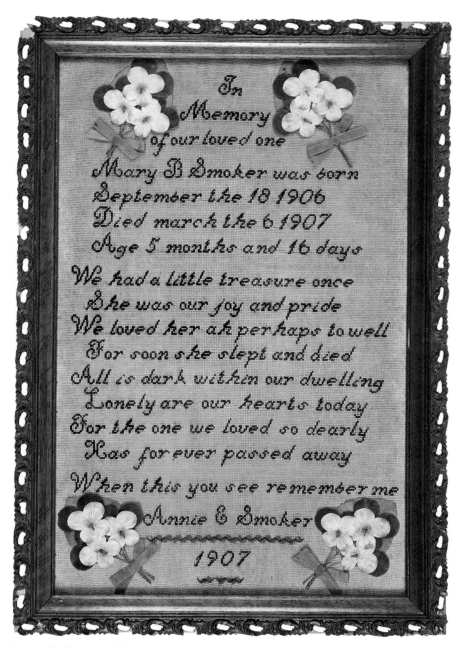

Memorial Sampler
Annie B. Smoker, 1907
17 1/4 × 25 1/2 including frame
Wool yarn on Berlin canvas,
original frame
Private collection

Annie B. Smoker (1891-1961) made this memorial sampler when she was 16 to mourn the death of her cousin Mary B. Smoker, who died as an infant. Annie miscounted the number of months from September to March and listed her cousin as 5 months of age, not 6.

This sampler illustrates several decorative changes taking place in the Amish community after 1900. The artificial flowers in the corners began to appear on memorial samplers and family records. At the time they were viewed as much fancier than stitched decoration. The stitched lettering is a modern script type, with slanted lettering that mimics handwriting or the calligraphy becoming popular. The frame is obviously modern and a significant departure from the simple examples used earlier to contain such work.

While visibly different from pre-1900 memorial and family record needlework, this sampler retains a basic format that is traditional: a measure of life down to number of days, a memorial verse, floral decoration and the personal note seen on samplers and door towels 80–100 years prior—"when this you see remember me."

Cat Needlepoint

Unattributed, circa 1890–1910
14 ¼ × 19 ½
Wool yarn on burlap, wool binding,
cotton backing
Maureen and Gregory McCauley

Needlepoint, common for cushion
tops, is an otherwise rare form of
Amish textile art. The importance
of this piece is enhanced by the use
of animal subjects. A well defined,
almost regal cat perches on a cushion in the center. The cat is surrounded by eight smaller animals
and birds, several of which have a
pleasingly folk appeal. The rabbit
and dogs are particularly reminiscent of homemade stuffed Amish
toys.

The brick-red background provides the piece with a vibrancy
common in Amish textiles. The
wide binding found on Old Order
quilts from Lancaster County
appears here, giving it an Amish
look. The inclusion of a backing
indicates the piece was made to be
displayed. It was used most recently
as a mat atop a sewing machine.
Conceivably this was the original
intent of the maker.

Parrot

Lydia (Mast) Zook, 1907
13½ × 16
Wool yarn on Berlin canvas,
velvet binding
Kathryn and Dan McCauley

The parrot is a popular motif appearing in Pennsylvania German decorative
arts through the 19th century.[4] Here the bird is presented in a format of classic
Amish composition. A vivid green parrot sitting on a bright tree branch is
complemented by a very dark background. The black and green outer border is
used to focus attention on the subject.

The use of black velvet, an expensive fabric, for the binding signifies the
artist's attitude towards her work and the care with which her piece was conceived and executed. Colored borders, as an organizational tool, are seen
extensively in antique Amish textile art.

The subject increases the interest in this piece, since animals are rarely
chosen as motifs by Amish women. This fact does not appear to be related to
the taboo against creating graven images, but is simply a cultural peculiarity.
The women are instead flower- and garden-oriented. Since they produced the
textile arts, subjects related to their interests were the norm.[5]

Lydia Mast was born September 24, 1824, and married Jacob K. Zook on
November 26, 1846. She is reputed by her family to have been fond of needlework, especially in her later years. She was eighty-three when she designed
and executed this piece. It passed to a granddaughter after Lydia's death.

Twin Parrots
R.L. (Rebecca Lapp), 1867
7 ⅝ × 10 ¼
Wool yarn on punched cardboard
Kathryn and Dan McCauley

Parrots were frequently seen on Pennsylvania German fraktur. Likely this artist was exposed to these designs, possibly in the home of a non-Amish neighbor, and then decided to use them in a work of her own. She chose colors that reflected her Amish heritage.

Rebecca (Lantz) Lapp made this piece in 1867 when she was twenty-eight and expecting her fourth child, Daniel. That she engaged in needlework during the most active period of her married life indicates her particular commitment to creativity. Her enthusiasm may have influenced her children, Henry and Elizabeth (Lizzie), both of whom are recognized Amish artists. A number of Rebecca's works have survived, several of which are included in this book, suggesting she was a fairly prolific textile artist.

Her parrots hung in a private area of her home and did not receive public display. Several related drawings attributed to Henry or Lizzie have survived and were most certainly based directly on this work. The needlework was inherited by a stepdaughter, Rebecca, as a namesake remembrance from Becky Lapp. It remained in the possession of this stepdaughter until purchased from her estate.

Needlework picture
Maria Stoltzfus, 1838
16 × 16 ¾
Wool thread on homespun linen
Private collection

According to her birth record (page 129), Mary Stoltzfus was born June 20, 1827, to John and Catharine (Hooley) Stoltzfus. She completed her needlework picture when she was eleven years old.

Overall, the composition is balanced and consistent in style with other early Amish works. Mary's name and the year are contained within a floral frame surrounded by twenty finely-stitched, multi-colored motifs. Like most pre-1860 needlework from eastern Pennsylvania, this piece is typically Pennsylvania German. Only the artist's name indicates that it is an Amish work.

Mary was the daughter of "Tennessee" John Stoltzfus, one of the nationally recognized leaders of the more liberal faction in Lancaster County. She married David Beiler, Jr., the son of Bishop David Beiler, the head of the conservative group. Mary's husband was ordained into the ministry in 1866 and eventually replaced his father as one of the most influential conservative leaders in the Lancaster Amish community.

*Fammals of
Christian and Rebeca Byler
Christian Byler was born september
th 8 th 1811
Rebeca Stolzfus was born augustt
th 2 th 1816
David F Byle was born december
th 25 th 1834
Anna Byler was born october
th 9 th 1836
Elesabeth Byler was born december
th 7 th 1838
Rebeca Byler was born november
th 8 th 1840
Christian Byler was born augustt
th 1 th 1842
Catharine Byler was born april
th 11 th 1844
Susanna Byler was born november
th 1 th 1846
John C Byler was born augustt
th 9 th 1848
Jonas F Byler was born september
th 20th 1850
Samuel L Byler was born febuary
th 8 th 1853
Benjamin F Byler was born febuary
th 25th 1855
Sarah Byler was born september 15 1857
C B 1863*

Family Record
CB (Catherine Byler), 1863
21 ⁷⁄₈ × 25 ³⁄₄ (including frame)
Wool yarn on punched cardboard,
original cherry frame
Private collection

Punched board became a popular base for sampler work among the Amish during the 1850s. Gradually it was replaced by canvas, probably because the cardboard dried out, becoming brittle. In addition, paper-based work was easily damaged, making finished pieces hard to store.

Use of the wandering vine to organize and contain sampler work was popular with the Amish until needlework family records fell from fashion after the first quarter of the 20th century, when they were replaced by calligraphy.

Cherry frames similar to this one accompany many works from this period and may have been provided by an Amish craftsman. Such pieces are illustrated in *A Craftsman's Handbook*, the design catalog of the Amish cabinet-maker Henry Lapp. The ring hangers, the use of cherry wood and the simple clear design of these pieces indicate an Amish creator.

Catherine executed this work at the age of nineteen, shortly before she married David Glick. It was probably a gift to her parents before she left home. She reacquired it upon her mother's death in 1902. Curiously, she spelled the family name "Byler," a midwestern version, as opposed to the "Beiler" popularly used in Lancaster County. Catherine signed and dated her work at the bottom. It is interesting that Amish samplers and drawings were commonly signed whereas almost all other decorative arts were not. Signing one's work seems to have been considered "prideful"; samplers appear to be an exception to this rule

Center Square
Susan Ebersol, circa 1910
79×79
Wool
Private collection

The Center Square pattern is far less common among Lancaster Amish quilt-makers than the similar Center Frame, which originated in the Midwest. The Center Square appears to have been most favored in the late 19th century, before it was modified by the placement of a diamond into the center. This variation became so popular that by the 1920s it had replaced the simpler design.

The quilt shown here is believed to have been made by Susan Ebersol shortly before her death in 1914. However, she died young and her son may have been given his mother's dowry quilt when he left home. This would explain the 1910 date on a quilt typical of those made around 1890.

The lily blossoms in the center field are very rare on Amish quilts.

The Amish designation of "saya" or "saw" quilt has caused collectors to refer to this pattern as a Sawtooth Diamond. It is basically a Center Diamond design to which strips of half blocks are added to effect the saw. Sawtooth Diamond quilts are generally composed of two contrasting colors, Center Diamonds of three or more. The outer border of this example is more narrow than generally encountered, a feature sometimes found on early pieces.[6] Corner squares are frequently found on this pattern.

The diamond center is quilted with a large, vibrating star with eight pin-wheel flowers filling the spaces between the arms; the diamond corners are filled with scallop quilting. The purple inner saw border has pinwheels between chevrons.

Sawtooth Diamond
Unattributed, circa 1890–1915
76 × 76½
Wool
Judy Boisson

41

Sawtooth Diamond Variation
Unattributed, circa 1890–1920
82 × 84
Wool
Susen and Jay Leary

A most unusual variation of the traditional sawtooth pattern, this quilt uses a third color in the outer border, giving it considerably more definition.

Light grey as the central background allows the red "saw" diamond to make a bold impression. The purple outer border cools the quilt and does not draw the eye away from the center. Bright red as a binding not only mirrors the saw, but clearly defines the edge of the quilt.

This quilt is significant as an interim step between the traditional Center Diamond and the apparently derivative Sawtooth Diamond design. It also shows how subtle changes in Amish motifs, like the use of a third color as seen in the outer border, radically affect the graphic impact of a quilt. And it gives witness to the power and sophistication of simple geometric designs.

The positioning of teal blue against deep red and an abundance of masterful quilting combine here to produce an exceptional quilt. The lyre-shaped feather scrolls in the center diamond are skillfully placed to emphasize the diamond design, while the long trailing vine in the sawtooth vines border aids in projecting the illusion of the square.

Sawtooth Diamond
Unattributed, circa 1920–1925
82×82
Wool
Lorraine and Paul Wenrich

Floating Center Diamond
Fannie (Stoltzfus) Fisher, circa 1910–1915
74 × 74
Wool
Private collection

Here all the hallmarks of an early quilt are present: simple but bold design; prolific, well detailed quilting; small size; and traditional Amish colors. An eight-pointed star within a large feather wreath is quilted in the central diamond field. The corners of the diamond are filled with pumpkin seed flowers. The inner border has swirling feather vines ending in tulip flowers.

The absence of corner squares gives the center diamond the appearance of floating. The decision not to include corner blocks resulted in a sophisticated composition. The dark maroon center and inner borders stand out against the light blue-grey outer border. The contrast projects a sense of boldness and power commonly encountered in good Lancaster Amish quilts. The positioning of very bright against very dark colors is a feature integral to many of the best Lancaster pieces.

Fannie Fisher made this piece for her daughter Lydia's hope chest, along with a set of hand-embroidered pillow cases. Among the first items to be "put up" for Lydia's dowry, they symbolized her transition from child to young adult.

44

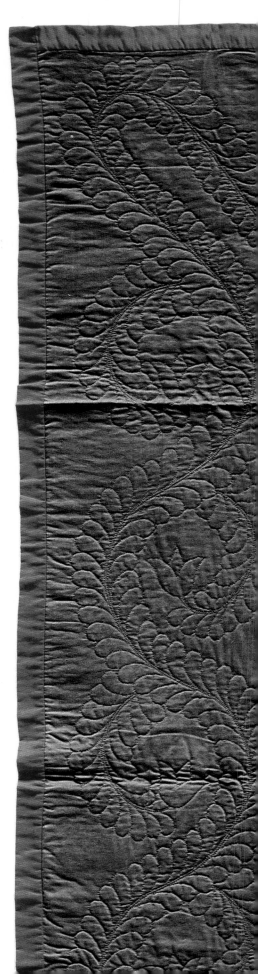

Center Diamond with
Nine Patch Center
Unattributed, 1900–1910
72 × 72
Wool
Esprit Quilt Collection

Not satisfied with the traditional Floating Diamond, this seamstress improved the design by filling the center with nine-patch blocks. A unique adaptation, this pattern is one of only two examples known. Both appear to have originated from the same hand.

An appreciation for color balance is evidenced by the selection of earth-tones to separate the intense red outer border from the violet nine-patch field. The symmetrical positioning of these hues keeps the dominant colors from clashing.

A meticulous rendering of classic quilting patterns combines with innovative design and skillful use of color to produce a striking work of Amish textile art.

Possibly a unique combination of two traditional patterns, this piece is exceptionally well composed and graphic. The soft, deep outer border and diamond inner borders are contrasted against bright Sunshine and Shadow piecework. The seamstress mirrored her center design in the four bordering triangles. The diamond shape is reflected in both the inner field and wine border, while the illusion of the square vibrates in from the inner border through the piecework. None of the fabrics used is especially bright; however, their skillful positioning results in such an impression.

Center Diamond/Sunshine and Shadow Combination
Unattributed, 1930–1940
86 × 86
Wool, cotton, crepe
Susen and Jay Leary

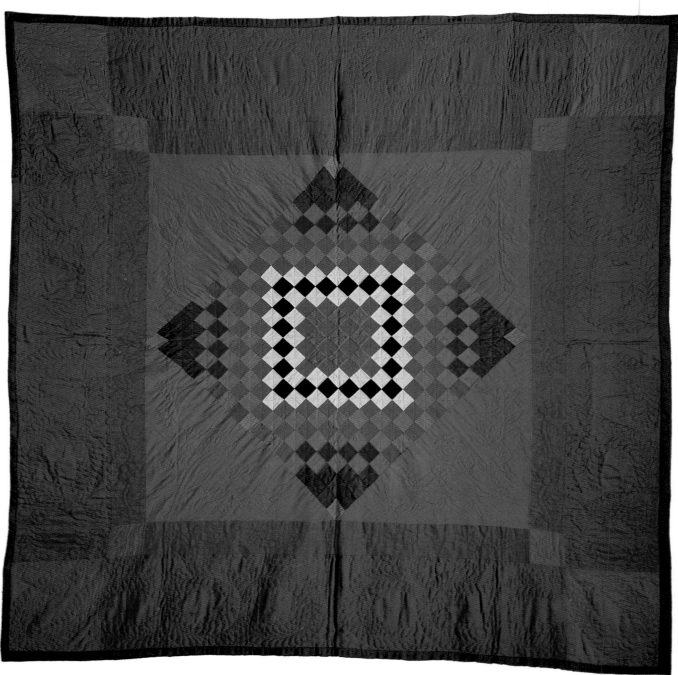

Center Diamond with Sunshine and Shadow Center
Sadie Lapp, circa 1900–1915
82×82
Wool
Barbara Janos

Combining the Center Diamond with the Sunshine and Shadow design produced a popular variation of both patterns. This example has corners in both the outer and inner borders. The blue in the binding is carried through the corners into the triangles.

Sadie chose to use a subdued violet for the wide outer border. This provides a subtle contrast which does not detract from the multi-colored piecework in the center. The bright red inner border focuses the eye on the piecework.

Like many wool dowry quilts, this piece survived in mint condition—most likely because it was reserved for display on the guest room bed once a year when the family hosted church. Otherwise it was stored, neatly folded, in a blanket chest, possibly to be used if special guests came to call.

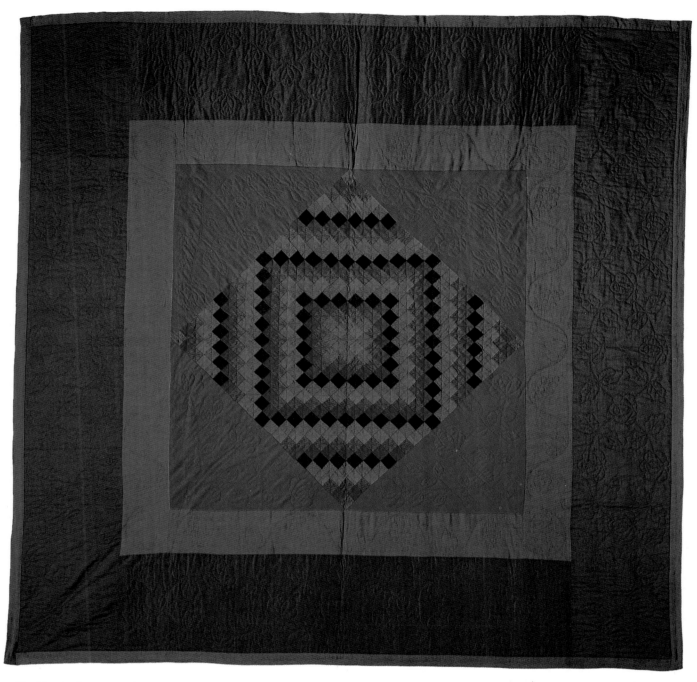

Similar in design to the previous example, this quilt lacks corner squares, allowing the diamond to float. The predominance of dark hues in the piecework set against a blue inner and dark green outer border gives this piece a serene tone. The red triangles add life to the quilt and a spark of color that lifts the piece above the mundane.

The wide green outer border is filled with rose wreath quilting. The vine theme is continued in the inner border with the grapevines and into the center with the rose branches in the red triangles.

Center Diamond with Sunshine and Shadow Center
Unattributed, circa 1925–1935
74 × 74
Wool and crepe
Esprit Quilt Collection

The Sunshine and Shadow center of this quilt is composed of over 1500 blocks and twenty-five hues of color. An organized dark and light shading is consistently maintained. The wide, burgundy outer border is quilted with Penn's feathers, terminating in tulip-flower finials. A soft blue binding defines the edge of the quilt without drawing the eye away from the graphics in the center.

Fannie Fisher made this piece for her daughter Sylvia in 1937 or 1938. Sylvia remembers sitting patiently with her mother on several occasions while they carefully selected colors to go in the center. They shifted material back and forth until exactly the desired image resulted. Weeks of planning passed before any sewing began. From start to finish, working in her spare time, it took Fannie a year to complete her project.

Sunshine and Shadow
Fannie Fisher, 1937–1938
82 × 82
Wool and cotton
Maureen and Gregory McCauley

While crepe Sunshine and Shadow quilts became ubiquitous in Lancaster County after 1940, early wool quilts in this pattern are fairly rare.[7] This example was made by Susie Petersheim for her daughter Sarah about 1920. Many of the colors popular among the Lancaster Amish at the time are present in the piecework. Black pieces are sometimes encountered in Sunshine and Shadow quilts, but as a rule black is rare in Lancaster Amish quilts, as opposed to the midwestern communities where it was commonly used.

The aqua inner border defines and organizes the multi-patch field. The use of navy for the outer border complements the piecework and focuses attention on the patterning in the Sunshine and Shadow composition. The maroon tape binding defines the edge of the quilt and organizes the entire presentation.

Sunshine and Shadow
Attributed to Susie Petersheim,
circa 1920
73 × 73
Wool
Kathryn and Dan McCauley

51

Sunshine and Shadow
Arie (Fisher) Esh, circa 1925–1930
81×81
Wool
Barbara Janos

Arie Fisher was born in 1881 and married in 1902. She and her husband, Amos Esh, had six children. In 1908 Amos was ordained a minister in the Middle Pequea district. Arie made this quilt about 1928 for her son Daniel, who was preparing to marry Susie Fisher.

Red and pink dominate the color scheme of the quilt. To keep her work from appearing garish, Arie chose to use a subtle tan for the corner squares and inner border squares.

The tulips quilted in the corners are usually found on older pieces, while the baskets and grapevines are frequently found on pieces made between 1910 and 1940.

Jacobina Stoltzfus (1859–1920) was the daughter of John Stoltzfus (1810–1897) and Elizabeth (Nafziger) Stoltzfus (1820–1907). She was named for her maternal grandmother, Jacobina (Swartzentruber) Nafziger (1793–1869), who had immigrated to America in 1827.

Presumably Jacobina made, or was given, this quilt for her dowry between 1875 and 1880. The piecework contains an unprecedented amount of patterned calico fabric for the Lancaster Amish. The green corners and maroon outer border are color coordinated to the piecework by the inclusion of scraps of the same material in the Courthouse Steps design. For the binding, gray felt was brought around to the face and sewn down. The corners are quilted with tulips and the outer border has fiddlehead ferns.

Log Cabin Quilt
Jacobina Stoltzfus, 1870–1880
72×79
Cotton
Kathryn and Dan McCauley

53

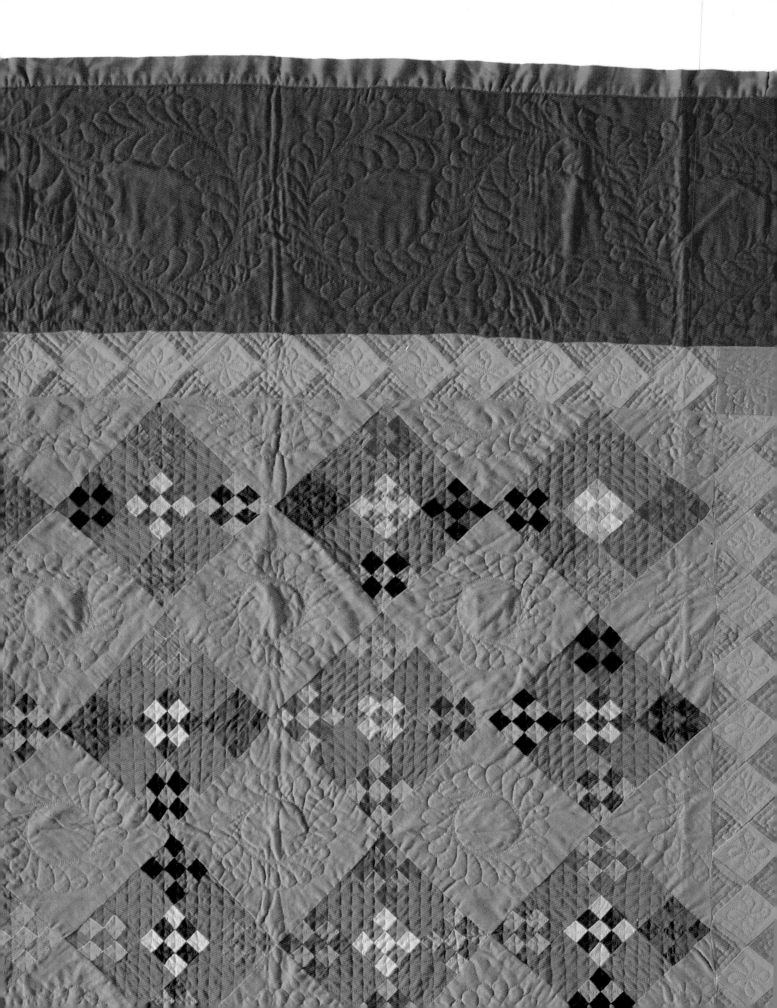

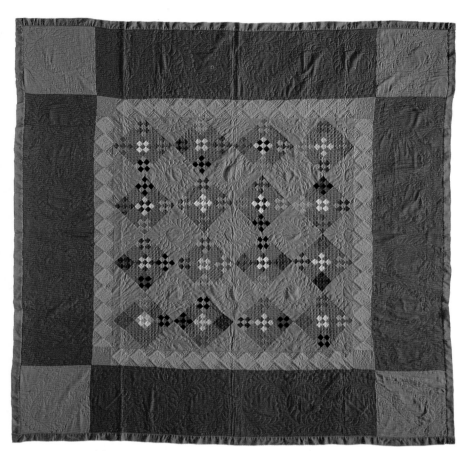

Double Nine-Patch
Unattributed, circa 1935–1945
87 × 87
Wool
Catherine H. Anthony

The Double Nine-Patch is one of only a few widely produced quilt designs that allowed for the use of a broad range of colors. This example was made for Aaron Beiler, probably between 1935 and 1945. Not only is it colorful, but the maker chose to enhance the design by including a diamond block inner border. Occasionally encountered on Double-Nine and Bar pattern quilts, the diamond block should not be considered a common border treatment in Lancaster Amish quilting. In this conservative community, bold alterations such as diamond or multiple-pieced inner borders were not widely accepted.

The blue background squares in the center are repeated in the large and small corner squares. Purple dominates the nine-patch squares and corresponds well to the lavender inner border. The green diamonds are exaggerated, as is the entire center of the quilt, by the use of a dark outer border. It serves almost as a picture frame and allows the interior colors to glow against it. The use of aqua for the binding and lavender in the borders demonstrates the move toward pastel shades beginning to take place in the Amish community at this time.

Double Nine-Patch
Attributed to Nancy Diener Riehl,
circa 1953
84 × 84
Wool, cotton and rayon
Catherine H. Anthony

Nancy Diener was born on December 29, 1883. She married Gideon Riehl in 1903, and they had ten children. In 1953, the year she reached 70 and her namesake granddaughter was preparing a dowry, Nancy made this quilt.

A somewhat later piece than the other items in this book, this quilt is included because it demonstrates how gradually change takes place among the Amish. Many mothers during this period were making Sunshine and Shadow quilts out of crepe and other synthetics. Pastel and shiny, "1950s" fabrics were being widely accepted by both young girls and their mothers. Yet some quilts, probably made by the older women, continued to be fashioned in traditional fabrics and colors. If it were not for the use of a few pieces of rayon crepe, this piece could be adjudged much earlier than the 1950s.

Although the Fence Row pattern is common in Lancaster County, historically it was almost unknown in the area's Amish community. Here it has been fit into the classic Amish format utilizing the group's preferred colors, wide outer border, quilting motifs and accentuated tape binding. This is a stellar example of an Amish adaptation of popular taste to reflect group preferences and values.

Rebecca (Lantz) Lapp married into the Stoltzfus family after the premature death of her husband, Michael Lapp. She made this quilt for the dowry of her stepdaughter Annie Stoltzfus shortly before Annie's marriage to Jacob Glick in the winter of 1892. Other innovative textile creations from Rebecca's hands have survived.

Fence Row
Rebecca (Lantz) Lapp, circa 1890
72 × 81
Wool
Private collection

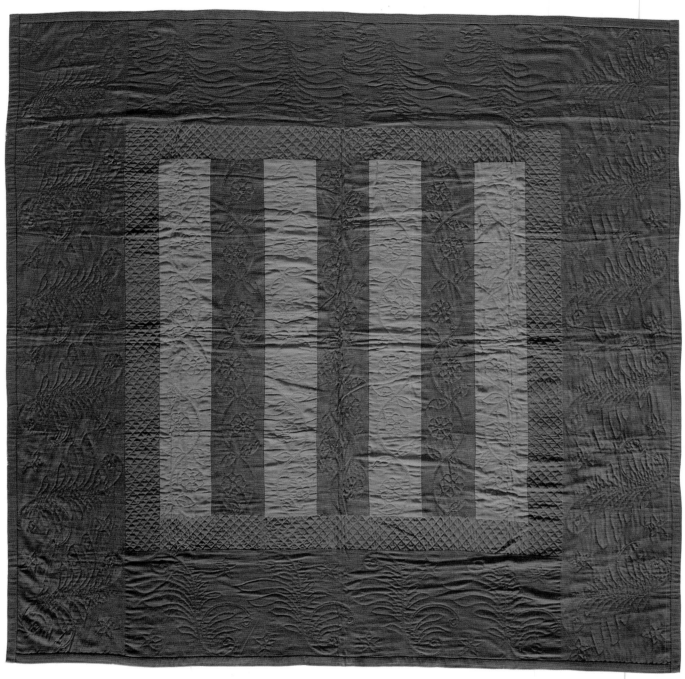

Floating Bars
Unattributed, circa 1930
79 × 79
Wool
McCauley Law Offices

The Amish often call this a Strip quilt, while collectors call the pattern Floating Bars. The absence of corner squares in the wide outer border, which ordinarily serve to anchor the central field to the binding, explains this quilt's name.

The purple used here was a popular dress color during the 1930s, but the shades of green and blue were not commonly used in dresses and were probably purchased specifically for quilt-making. While the green is a lime shade and corresponds well to the violet and blue, the overall impact is softer than encountered in many examples. By binding the quilt in the same purple as is used in the outer border, the maker induces the viewer to focus on the central field.

Basically a combination of square and rectangular shapes, the Bar quilt is one of the geometric patterns that evolved in the Lancaster Amish community during the 19th century. The broad expanses of fabric rendered by the large geometric shapes served as backdrops to be enhanced by prolific and meticulously executed quilting stitches.

Sarah Esh Stoltzfus (1863–1917), the wife of the Amish Bishop Samuel Stoltzfus, made this quilt for her daughter Hannah about 1915. One of nineteen children, Hannah married John Stoltzfus in 1921. When an Amish settlement began in St. Mary's County, Maryland, in 1940, John moved the family south rather than submit to governmental pressure to send his children to a large, consolidated public school.

Bars
Sarah (Esh) Stoltzfus, circa 1915
81 × 84
Wool
Private collection

Bars
Unattributed, circa 1880–1895
72 × 82 ¼
Wool
Judi Boisson

This pattern is known among the Amish as a "Stramma" or "Strip" quilt. This example is a masterpiece of early Amish quilt design.

The inclusion of corner blocks in a quilt significantly affects its graphics. They join the inner border to the binding, enhancing the sense of activity in the design by carrying it from the center to the edge of the quilt.

The inner border is a device commonly used by Amish seamstresses to organize the piecework in the center. Here small diamonds decorate the inner border in a successful attempt to increase the quilt's visual appeal. Decorative features such as these diamonds are uncommon; usually the border is highlighted through quilting rather than piecework.

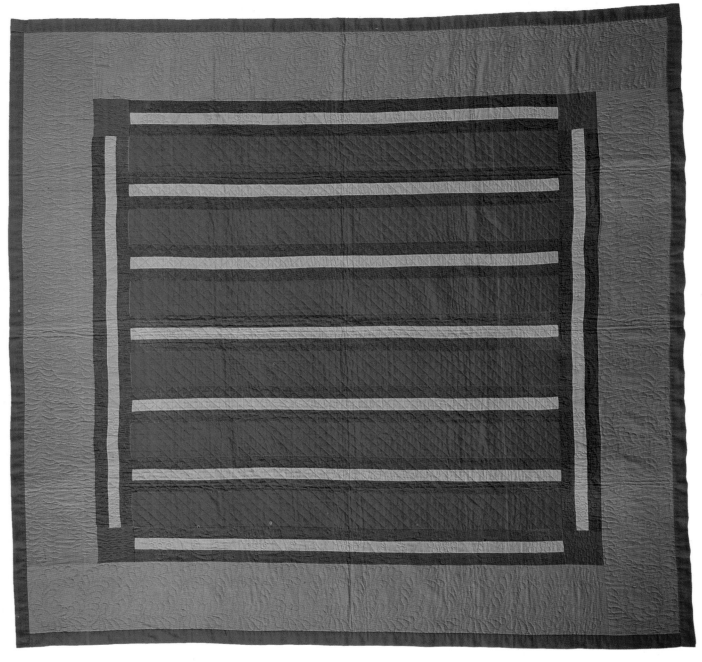

A variation of the Bars quilt, the split pattern is rare. This example is high-lighted by the split inner border, a very unusual modification. The yellow-gold bars stand out boldly against the deeply saturated wool fabric. The solid red bars, corner pieces and tape binding, usually strong design features on Lancaster County quilts, are subdued in this case by the powerfully graphic, yellow striped bars.

The scale of the central field is larger than normal, shrinking the size of the outer border and increasing the dominance of the multicolored bar theme.

The outer border is feather-quilted, while the inner split border has grape-vine quilting. The bar is waffle-quilted.

Split Bars
Unattributed, circa 1920
78 × 80
Wool
Esprit Quilt Collection

Triple Irish Chain
Lydia Petersheim, 1920–1925
82 × 83
Wool
Private collection

This typical example of Lancaster Amish Irish Chain patterns has no inner border. Instead, the maker applied an extraordinarily large binding to define the perimeter of the quilt. To highlight the fields between the piecework chain, she quilted feather wreaths containing eight-pointed stars. The outer border and corner squares are covered with scrolling "Penn" or "Quaker" feather quilting.

The backing of the quilt is a bright red, slightly ribbed silk. The quilting stands out on this background with such definition that the quilt was sometimes displayed on the bed facedown.

Lydia Petersheim crafted this piece for her namesake granddaughter, Lydia Kauffman, between 1920 and 1925. They went together to the fabric store in New Holland to select the material. As a rule the dowry quilts of the Lancaster Amish were not scrap quilts. The design and color were decided upon and then the material carefully selected to satisfy compositional requirements.

Almost without exception Amish children were given one "good" quilt to take from home. No matter how poor the family, these quilts were made of wool, until the acceptance of synthetic fabrics about 1940. The 1950s saw a universal rejection of the use of wool in Lancaster County Amish quilts.

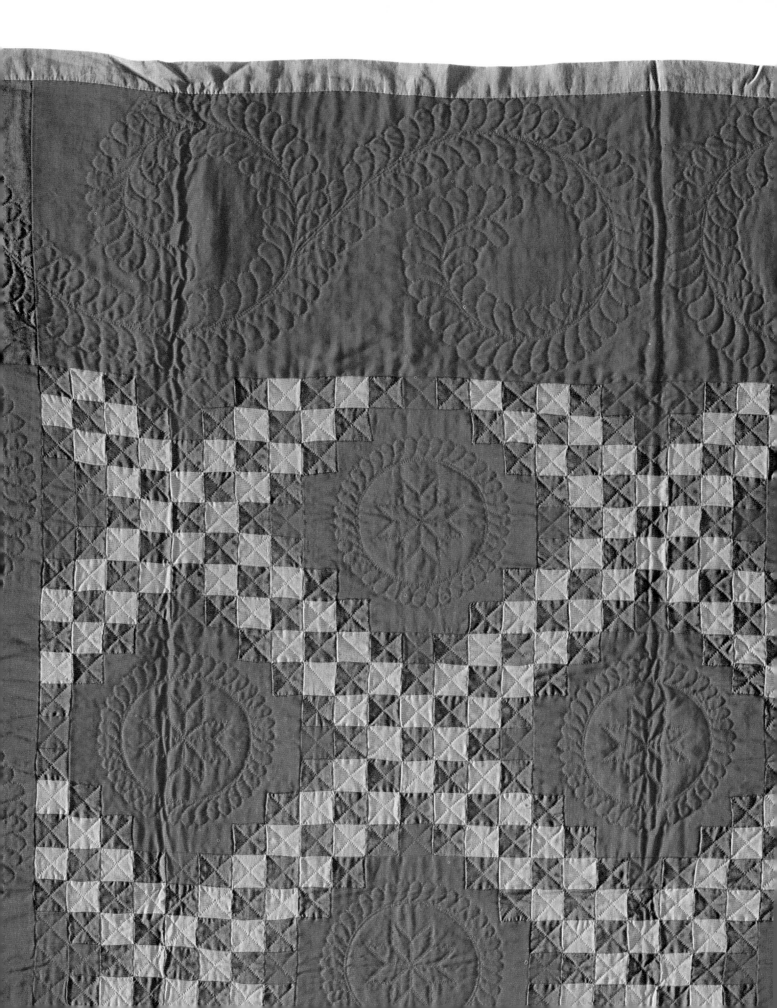

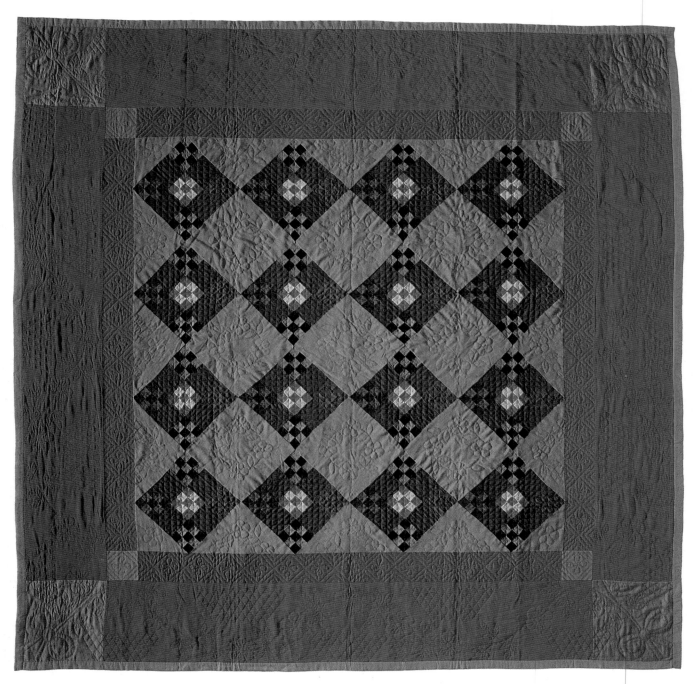

Nine-Patch
Annie L. Stoltzfus, circa 1920
82½ × 82½
Cotton
Private collection

Made as an everyday quilt about 1920, this piece is cotton instead of wool, which was expensive and usually reserved for "good" quilts.

Floral-vine quilting decorates both the inner and outer borders. A pattern sometimes encountered in early quilts, it became very popular after 1940. On later pieces the quilting tends to be sparse and less defined than that presented here. As a rule of thumb, the less prolific the quilting and the larger the quilt, the more recent the year of execution. Quilts larger than 82 inches square likely originated after 1920, and those 84 inches or larger about 1940.

Everyday quilts were often used as covers for sofas or daybeds. Many wore out in this capacity and were cut up for carpet rags, used to line comforters or made into batting for new quilts.

Nine Patch blocks are arranged on edge in the central field to produce a single Irish Chain variation. The quilt's colors were originally bright pink, light denim blue and deep green, but have softened after generations of use. This piece has little if any filling or batting, so it is thin and lightweight. The minute stitches in the quiltwork, ten to an inch, remain clearly visible despite the quilt's 100 years of use.

Eva Graver married Jacob Stoltzfus about 1865. She gave this quilt to her son Jacob when he married Barbara Nafziger. The quilt was already several years old when Jacob received it. The quality of this quilt testifies to the effort the Amish put into their work, even an "everyday" piece meant for hard use.

Nine Patch
Eva (Graver) Stoltzfus, 1870–1890
76×80
Cotton, homespun tick backing
Private collection

Sixteen-Patch

Attributed to Rebecca (Lantz) Lapp,
circa 1870–1880
74 × 77
Cotton denim and cotton
Anne and Bob Klemeyer

A very early quilt, this is one of only a few denim pieces to survive. It descended through the family of artists Henry and Lizzie Lapp and was probably crafted by their mother, who created a number of unusual textile works.

Sophisticated in composition, this quilt has multiple inner borders, not commonly done in Lancaster. The extensive use of orange is rare, as is the sixteen-patch pattern. The outer border is quilted with a tulip motif that appears to have been used on 19th century midwestern Amish quilts. The shift in Lancaster to darker colors took place about the time of the Civil War, partially as a result of the development of colorfast fabrics.

This "Kavli" or Basket quilt is similar to a number of other pieces that have been discovered. The seamstress who fashioned this example made an important contribution to knowledge about Lancaster quilts. In the border she initialed her work, "D L," for the owner Daniel Lapp, and dated it 1931. The pink-hued baskets are crepe, documenting the use of this fabric for piecing as early as that year.

Initials and dates in the border are common on midwestern Amish quilts but far rarer in Lancaster. More often in Lancaster, the initials of the owner were inconspicuously cross-stitched into a corner on the reverse side.

The graphics and color composition on this piece project an impression of strength. The piecing is finely executed; all corners meet and are sharp.

Baskets
Unattributed, 1931
79 × 80
Cotton, crepe
Susen and Jay Leary

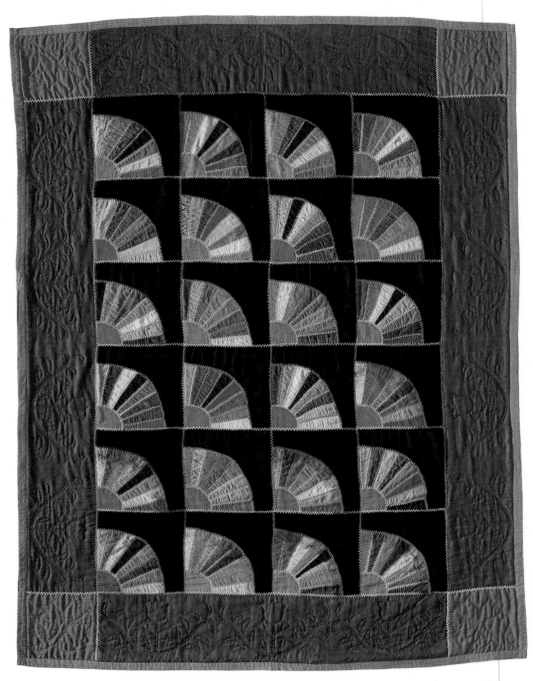

Fan Quilt
Flaud family, 1900–1920
56×72
Wool
Rachel and Kenny Pellman

Fan pattern quilts were popular in the mid-western Amish settlements, but are relatively unknown in the Lancaster community. Visible in this example is not only this rare piecework pattern but a possibly unique tulip bush quilting design in the outer border. The tulip stem in the corner squares is an early design abandoned after about 1920.

The use of black as a background is very rare in Lancaster quilts. Here it serves to allow the multi-colored fans to capture attention. The embroidery stitch used to highlight the piecing combines with the color selection to give the impression of a Victorian-era crazy quilt. The wide outer border, corner squares, color selection and tape binding provide the format that identify it as Amish in origin.

A pattern popular throughout midwestern settlements, the Eight-Pointed Star is all but unknown in Lancaster County, making this example an exceptionally uncommon quilt. It has the small size and captivating use of subdued color often encountered on early pieces. The designer increased the scale of the central field, thereby reducing the width of the outer border. The result is an enhanced domination of the star motif.

The use of tan striping between the star blocks introduces a sense of organization and permits them to stand out, increasing their strength. The corner squares extend this sense of order into the outer border. The dark tape binding does not draw the eye from the center.

Eight-Pointed Star
Unattributed, circa 1900–1920
78 × 78
Wool, cotton
Susen and Jay Leary

Lone Star
Unattributed, circa 1930–40
88 × 91
Wool, cotton
Susen and Jay Leary

The Lone Star is a rare Lancaster Amish pattern and is another example of a common "English" motif adapted to conform to Amish Design.[8]

The star is placed on a turquoise central field; an inner border is omitted to eliminate a crowded presentation. The wide outer border, exaggerated tape binding and color selection are purely Lancaster Amish features onto which the star has been superimposed.

Graphically, the star appears to be an eight-pointed blue sunburst to which darker arms have been added. The illusion draws the eye to the center and then shoots it to the black tips of the star. This is accomplished by the skillful use of dark saturated fabrics in the outer half, which contrast strongly with the lighter blues in the center. The overall effect is one of action and movement.

A well planned and sophisticated work, this quilt also shows the seamstress's creativity in its quilting. In the four corners of the inner field, between the arms, are quilted large vibrating stars which emphasize the theme. Formatted in cool, muted colors, this piece testifies to the Amish ability to accomplish bold graphics without relying entirely on manipulating strong, bright hues.

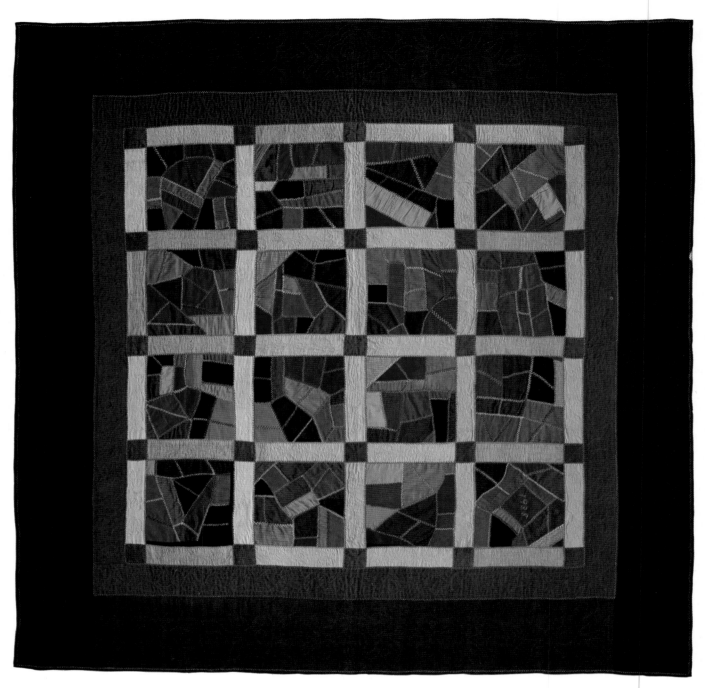

Crazy Patch
Unattributed, dated 1938
81 × 82
Wool and crepe
Esprit Quilt Collection

Crazy Patch quilts are common among the Amish. Essentially they are a variation of the simple Nine-Patch pattern with crazy squares replacing the patchwork. The color selection in the borders carefully reduces the contrast in this piece, resulting in a less traditional look.

The Amish designed their crazy quilts with the same restraint evidenced in their other patterns. Here the artist placed brightly colored crazy patches on a grid of lavender with purple joint squares. The deep teal inner border subtly contrasts against the green outer border. The top right-hand crazy patch is dated 1938, probably the year the quilt was completed.

The seamstress chose to use light thread, unusual in Lancaster, to emphasize the designs in her quilting.

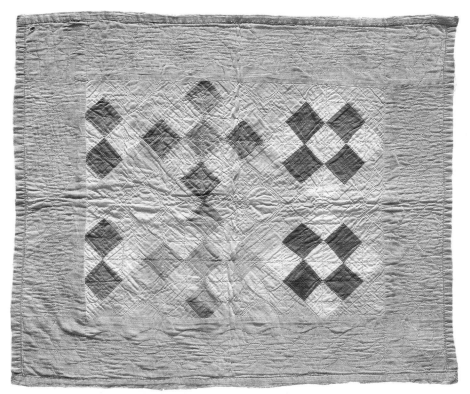

Nine Patch Crib Quilt
Unattributed, 1880–1910
30 × 35
Cotton
Private collection

While this appears to be miniaturized version of a full-size bed cover, the seamstress failed to scale down her Nine Patch blocks. Consequently, she had to settle for half blocks to fill the inner field.

Like almost all Amish quilts, the top is machine-sewn while the quilting is hand-rendered. The outer border is a home-dyed blue that has softened to a grayish cast. The binding is tan, a popular dress color in the 19th century. The pink squares between the nine-patch blocks are enhanced with an unusual "sun" motif.

Chinese Coin Crib Quilt
Unattributed, circa 1910
34½ × 40
Wool, cotton
Private collection

Early Amish crib quilts are rarely encountered among the Lancaster community. Blankets and bedspreads were the bedcovers of choice for cribs and trundle beds. One reason for this lack of popularity may be that wool was the choice fabric for quilts and did not hold up to the repeated washing and cleaning required of infant bedcoverings.

The Chinese Coin pattern is extremely rare in Lancaster. The maker of this quilt modified the design by making her coins in a crazy quilt arrangement.

This is a genuine "scrap" quilt. The piecing contains many early dress fabrics. The preponderance of blue, violet/purple and brown is consistent with the Ordnung regarding dress colors in Lancaster at the turn of the century.

73

Hooked Rug with Doves
Unattributed, circa 1880–1920
19½ × 40
Cotton on burlap
Barbara Janos

Morning doves or lovebirds were a
relatively common subject in Pennsylvania German art. Although not
frequently used by the Amish, they
appear in this outstanding example
of the pattern. Set on a deep violet
background, two aqua doves are
perched on branches at either end of
a multicolored field of blooms. The
black scalloped border was common
on early Amish pieces, as was the
contrasting lighter outline.

"The Team" Hooked Rug
Salome Stoltzfus, circa 1935–1945
23½ × 42
Wool, burlap
Private collection

This design was developed by Aaron L. Smucker about 1930 for his sister,
Sarah, according to a letter which Sarah Smucker King wrote on June 27,
1985. The pattern quickly gained acceptance as a pattern for Amish boys'
rugs. All known examples are essentially the same, varying only in small
details. Some lack the birds, others the oval picture-frame border. Careful
examination of this piece shows that the background horse has no front legs.

The artist presents two major contrasts: the pastel inner field, defined by
the picture frame against the black outer border, and the vivid red-hued pansies against the entire surface. Both command attention, yet are so skillfully
orchestrated that no distraction is created.

As is true of many Amish rugs, the subject on this one is remarkably lifelike. There seemed to be two primary attitudes among the Amish in regard to those arts and crafts which included subjects from nature. Some members appear to have reasoned that since only God is perfect, human creation should not attempt too close a likeness to what God has made.[9] Others seemed to believe that one's work should appear as real and close to the original as possible.[10]

Mary Fisher apparently subscribed to the latter understanding. Her swan is lifelike and well detailed. The water is highlighted with dark blue to suggest movement. Her selection of pink water lilies, which enhance the corners of the rope border, completes the pond theme. A black frame with a single white border serves to organize the piece.

Hooked Rug with Swan
Attributed to Mary Fisher, circa 1935
23¼ × 29¾
Cotton on burlap
Barbara Janos

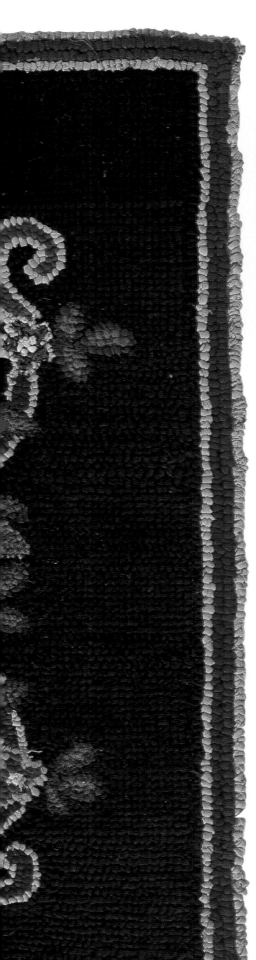

Floral Hooked Rug
Emma Beiler, 1935
25½ × 26½
Cotton on burlap
Kathryn and Dan McCauley

Called a "Forget-me-not" rug because of the flowers used to decorate it, this pattern was very popular between 1920 and 1935. The use of hot pink, deep maroon and electric green on a black background make this a startling graphic piece. It shows that the Amish women's penchant for contrasting bold and dynamic colors dominated their textile arts.

    Emma made this piece for her dowry. She chose much of the material specifically for her rugs; little is scrap dress fabric except the black which was from worn-out dresses and aprons. Men's clothing was not used for rugs because the material was too heavy and did not "rug" well.

Hooked Rug with Flower Basket
Emma Blank, circa 1935–1940
24 ¾ × 27 ¼
Cotton on burlap
Private collection

Hooked rugs are made by stretching jute or burlap feed sacks on a wooden frame. A pattern is drawn on the foundation, then filled in with yarn or thread that is drawn through the burlap. A slow, tedious process, it takes many women as long to finish a rug as it does to make a quilt.

The basket of flowers proved to be a very popular pattern among the Old Order women. Pansies, as appear here, were often the flowers of choice, but petunias are also seen. The bright red used to highlight the basket draws attention to the center.

Made by Emma Blank about the time she married into the King family in 1938, this rug shows a "modern" look in the design of the floral border. The preponderance of aqua and the pastels used for the flowers support the impression that this was a later Amish work.

Flower Basket Hooked Rug
Sylvia Fisher, circa 1925–1930
26½ × 39½
Cotton, wool and burlap
Private collection

Hooked rugs, like most Amish textile arts, reflect the values of the community. The majority of the components were salvaged, a sign of thrift. Worn garments and feed sacks were given a second life. Designs and patterns were shared. However, individual expression is manifest, for the most part through color selection and modification of a basic pattern. In most pieces a harmonious balance between community and individuality is maintained.

Almost all rugs, despite design and color, have a common feeling or look due to the influence of the Ordnung. Women knew both consciously and unconsciously what was acceptable to the code of the Church and produced pieces within those parameters.

This flower basket rug was made by Sylvia Fisher for her dowry between 1925 and 1930. It is classic in both motif and color. The chain border is unusual but does not represent a radical departure from the traditional design for rugs. The Fisher family was fond of textile art. Each child received a quilt and at least two hooked rugs to take from home. The girls made a horse rug, showing a team, as a keepsake for each of their brothers.

Floral Hooked Rug
Emma Fisher, 1929
27 × 45½
Cotton on burlap
Private collection

A forget-me-not rug of similar pattern to the example on page 77, this piece shows how changes in color can make rugs of the same pattern visually different. The gray background softens the overall impression of this rug.

The piano-key border is an unusual enhancement of the pattern. A device encountered on Midwest Amish quilts, this border treatment is very rarely seen in Lancaster County Amish textile art. Emma used some printed fabric in the border to "brighten it up."

Stag Hooked Rug
Mary (King) Lapp, circa 1930
27 1/2 × 42
Cotton
Private collection

Mary (King) Lapp made this piece about 1930 for her husband. She drew her original pattern directly on the burlap. The scalloped shape is unique, as is her entire border treatment. Mary made a number of hooked rugs, almost all in traditional patterns and colors.

Home Sweet Home Hooked Rug
Circa 1890-1910
25 ¾ × 40 ¾
Wool, cotton and burlap
Private collection

This early rug is distinguished by a highly decorative floral chain border and the extensive use of patterned fabric and rug yarn. The black material probably originated from a worn mourning dress, the deep red and violet from Sunday dresses. The patterned material, bright red, pink and the faded lime green were contrary to the Ordnung for dress in Lancaster County; therefore, these colors were specifically obtained for making rugs.

Why bright colors were permitted in rugs and quilts is not clear. It does seem, however, that even in their textiles the Amish observed a set of unwritten rules. While patterned fabric is somewhat common in rugs, it is very rarely encountered in Amish quilts.

Squirrels are not commonly found in Amish handcrafts, with the exception of some drawings of squirrels done by Henry Lapp. The squirrels on this rug are perched facing each other between a small brown bush, a composition similar in arrangement to the bird-in-bush drawings produced in the community.

These squirrels are remarkably lifelike with detailed accents, especially in their multi-shaded bushy tails. The acorn border is a whimsical variation of the vine border seen throughout Amish textile art. While softer in color contrast than many pieces, the kelly green used to represent a lawn or grass is a classically bold shade.

Squirrels and Acorns Hooked Rug
Arie Fisher, circa 1935–1940
24 × 41
Wool, burlap
Private collection

Hooked Rug with Floral Design
Emma Beiler, 1930–1935
23½ × 42
Wool, cotton and burlap
Private collection

The flowers pictured on Lancaster rugs are almost always petunias, pansies, forget-me-nots and roses—the flowers commonly found in Amish gardens. The images are usually representational.

Yet many rugs are conceptual in design and color, as this piece demonstrates. The oak-leaf inner border is bold and electric. The vibrant red of the pansies balances the power of the oak leaves, while a thin, hot-pink border defines the edge of the gray field and increases the impact of the black edge.

The artist, Emma Beiler, made a number of other equally graphic pieces. Her works are well composed and well crafted and show an exceptional color sense.

Stairway Hooked Rug
Rebecca King, 1925–1935
25 × 37
Cotton on jute
Private collection

Hooked rugs are almost universally popular among the Lancaster Amish. The size of these floor coverings seems to be defined by the unwritten, subconscious confines of the Ordnung. Without exception, floor rugs are small-area in size, generally about 24 × 42. Room-size examples are nonexistent. Miniature rugs made to cover the treadle of a sewing machine or serve as a table or chair mat are known, but very rare.

This Stairway rug was made by Rebecca King about 1930. It uses one of the more popular geometric patterns among the Old Order. Rebecca decorated this piece with an unusual zig-zag outer border. The rose bouquets bordering the stairway are found as a quilting pattern in the corner squares of some quilts made about the same time. Rebecca outlined and highlighted her designs in white. This adds a sense of power to the piece, especially to the outer border.

Shooting Stars Rug

Mary Lantz, circa 1935
34 × 44
Cotton
Kathryn and Dan McCauley

The Shooting Star rug pattern has rarely been found. Here the shape of the stars implies action moving away from the center; the zigzag border emphasizes this sense of motion. Three plain braided borders contain the design and focus the eye. The overall effect is almost three-dimensional.

Mary Glick married Stephen Lantz, November 20, 1913. Fond of "rugging," she made several crocheted and braided rugs about 1935 for the dowries of each of her children. Through a series of unique designs, Mary attempted to make her crocheted pieces as visually appealing as hooked rugs.

A testimony to the change of taste developing in the Amish community about 1940, one of Mary's daughters never removed her rugs from her blanket chest. She considered them "too dark" and "old-fashioned." They were wrapped in newspaper for over forty years until literally uncovered in the 1980s.

Diamond Rug

Mary Lantz, circa 1935
25½ × 57
Cotton
Kathryn and Dan McCauley

This rug was made by Mary Lantz for the dowry of the daughter whose star rug is shown above. This piece is larger than the star rug and has more crocheted work and less braiding. The center is composed of four multi-colored squares tipped on end to become diamonds. While the center is a geometric play of squares and triangles, the borders feature rectangles. The black-speckled inner border is an obvious manifestation of this shape, and a close look at the outer "piano-key" edge reveals that each shade is also presented as a rectangle.

The center material was salvaged from adult dresses. Its somber hues dominate the rug. The lighter piano-key trim, made from children's clothes, brightens the piece and increases its appeal. Unique in both design and concept, this rug displays Mary Lantz's talent, ingenuity and artistic sensitivity.

Rag Doll

Fannie (Petersheim) Kauffman,
circa 1930–1935
Cotton; rag stuffing
Private collection

The pinafore apron and booties on the feet indicate that this doll was meant to represent a baby or young child. On earlier baby dolls, the dress would often cover the feet, just as actual infant dresses did.

Fannie (Petersheim) Kauffman made this doll in the 1930s for her daughters. The head has black fabric to represent hair. Underneath the black is a brightly colored and patterned fabric. The patterned fabric used for the arms can be seen continuing into the hands.

Like many old dolls, this piece has a tightly-stuffed rag body that has become hard from repeated washings.

Teddy Bear

King family
11½ inches tall
Straw-stuffed, commercially made
Kathryn and Dan McCauley

This bear was a gift to one of the King children from his aunt in 1936. It may not have been new at the time. According to oral family history, during the early 1940s the little King girls pestered their mother to make a baby doll for them. Anxious to satisfy the girls, Mother King reached into the toy box for the bear and made a dress for it. The children were happy and the bear served as a doll for several generations.

This example illustrates the Amish penchant for recycling items. Old clothes are cut up for carpets. Salt bags become dolls. Jute feed sacks make foundations for hooked rugs. As long as a use can be found for an item, it is kept in circulation.

To become less dependent on the outside world and to provide work for their own members, the Amish encouraged one another to provide goods needed by the community. Lizzie Lapp became widely known for making and selling dolls. This doll is one of a pair purchased from her about 1918 by Annie Stoltzfoos for Annie's daughters.[11]

The body and head of Lizzie's dolls are one unit to which the arms and legs are attached. The feet have applied denim boots. The hands are flat pieces of denim, stuffed with rags and sewn to make articulated fingers. The bodies of her dolls have a unique hourglass shape with a defined waist.

In keeping with the Amish taboo against graven images, Lizzie's dolls have no facial features.

Rag Doll
Lizzie Lapp, circa 1918
15 inches tall
Cotton feed sack with rag stuffing;
denim, original cotton dress
Kathryn and Dan McCauley

Rag Doll
Unattributed, circa 1908–1910
18 inches tall
Cotton stuffed with rags; original
cotton clothes
Kathryn and Dan McCauley

These garments on this doll document the style common among Amish children at the turn of the century. The pinafore, worn by young girls, matches the dress. A decorative pleat is sewn in the center. The sleeves have a tuck near the shoulder and the skirt has three tucks in a row starting an inch above the hem. Ostensibly these folds were practical features meant to be let out as the child grew. In reality they proved a decorative feature still very popular in many mid-western communities. The cuffs have a purely fashionable trim. On women's garments this trim was black velvet and was often repeated at the collar. A custom that began at least as early as 1890, it continued in fashion into the 1930s.

The black "hair" and denim hands, with stitched, articulated fingers, are common features in antique Lancaster County rag dolls. Amish rag dolls are traditionally faceless, probably to conform to the same biblical admonition against graven images which Amish ministers used to proscribe photographs in the 1860s.

This doll was made for Mary Fisher shortly after she was born on June 22, 1908, probably by her mother or one of her grandmothers. Mary married Jacob King in 1948. They were childless and upon her death, the doll was passed to a young namesake niece as a keepsake.

Twin Dolls
Unattributed, circa 1893–1895
Cotton; rag stuffing
Private collection

These dolls were made for Annie Lapp (1891–1983), probably by her mother, Mattie (Smoker) Lapp (1860–1934). Annie married John Miller in 1910. She kept the dolls so her four daughters could play with them.

The bodies for these dolls are single-piece construction. The arms, legs and head are one piece with the torso. The green dress is probably original, while the violet probably dates from the 1930s. (Annie's youngest daughter would have been ten years old in 1935.) Both dolls have black adult half-aprons and stocking feet.

Doll Quilt: *Center Diamond*
Katie Stoltzfus, circa 1935
15½ × 16¼
Wool
Private collection

Katie Stoltzfus made this doll quilt for her daughter about 1935. In color and pattern it could have been made considerably earlier, a testimonial to the traditional designs and values of this society. The quilt was handed down from Katie's daughter to her granddaughter.

The Center Diamond was one of the most widely produced patterns for full-sized bed quilts up until about 1940. Almost overnight it seems to have been replaced by the Sunshine and Shadow design. Although doll quilts are comparatively rare, the Sunshine and Shadow variations of the Four- and Nine-Patch patterns comprise most early surviving Lancaster examples. The Diamond pattern is seldom found.

Doll Quilt: *Bars*
Unattributed, circa 1930
16 × 19
Cotton
Wanda and Smith Johnson

Purchased from an Amish family in southern Lancaster County, this is an unusual treatment of the Bars design. The light colors and patterned fabric give the quilt an unusually soft appearance.

Machine quilting is common on Amish doll quilts. The navy blue thread on this piece was probably a conscious effort at contrast.

An examination of the back of the quilt reveals it to be a much earlier piece upon which a new top was sewn and binding added, probably in the late 1930s or '40s. It is not unusual for Amish quilts to have an earlier piece as their foundation.

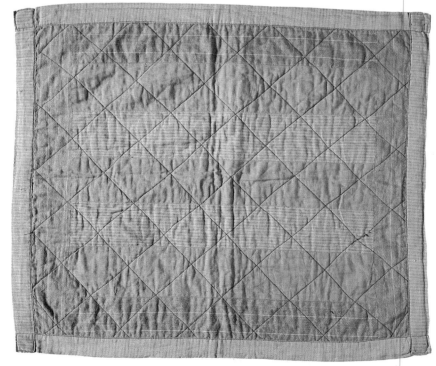

Doll Quilt: Crazy Quilt

Unattributed, circa 1880
14 ¾ × 23 ½
Wool, cotton embroidery,
cotton backing
Kathryn and Dan McCauley

Crazy *patch* quilts were made by the
Lancaster Amish, but *overall* crazy
designs, like the one pictured, were
primarily reserved for comforts—
thick, quilt-like bed covers which
were usually knotted, rather than
quilted.

Pre-1940 doll quilts from Lancaster are very rare and 19th century examples are almost unknown.
This piece descended through the
Stoltzfus family, but the precise
identity of the maker has been lost.

The quilting is a hand-embroidered stitch used to join the piecing.
Many other Amish doll quilts were
machine-quilted.

Doll Quilt: Checkerboard

King family, circa 1945–55
17 × 17
Cotton
Private collection

White was not broadly accepted as
a color in Amish quilts until the
1940s, when it became popular for
summer-weight pieces. Here it was
used for a doll quilt, one of a pair
made by a member of the King family for her daughters' doll beds. The
wide outer border and wide binding
found on full-size quilts are present
here. In addition, this hand-quilted
piece has a floral vine pattern in the
outer border and is accentuated by
blue thread.

Door Towel

Rebecca Lantz Lapp, 1855
15 ¾ × 53 ¼
Cotton embroidery on woven cotton,
applied mill-made fringe
Private collection

Long, hand-embroidered towels
were commonly made by Pennsylvania German girls to be hung on the
backs of their homes' guest-room
doors.[12] Since the towels were to be
viewed by house guests, many young
women utilized their best needlework skills when executing them.

Rebecca made this towel three
years before she married Michael
Lapp. She chose to decorate it in red
and green, a combination that
appears to have been popular with
the Amish in the 19th century.
While most of her motifs are associated with traditional Pennsylvania
German cultural influence, the
roosters have a decidedly "American" flavor, illustrating the effect of
extra-cultural ideas on the Amish.

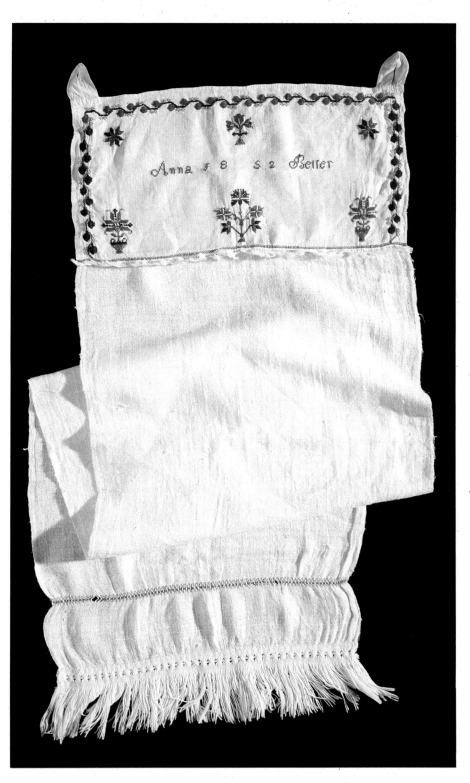

Door Towel
Annie Beiler, 1852
15¼ × 50
*Cotton thread embroidery on woven
cotton, applied mill-made fringe
Private collection*

While many Pennsylvania German
towels are profusely decorated,
Amish examples tend to conform to
the precept of simplicity. An overly
embellished piece would possibly
have been construed as a manifestation of pride. Annie's is a well
developed Amish piece. The design
is balanced and she included her
full name and the date along with
favored decorative motifs. She organized the entire presentation within
a detailed border.

Although decorated door towels
reached their zenith of popularity in
the Germanic community between
1820 and 1850,[13] it seems they were
most popular among the Amish
between 1850 and 1920.

Annie Beiler (1836–1915) completed her towel when she was six-
teen. From the surviving examples
it appears that Amish girls made
their towels between the ages of fif-
teen and eighteen, about the time
they were preparing a dowry for
marriage.

Bolster Cover
Annie K. Stoltzfus, circa 1890
21 ¼ × 56
Cotton thread embroidery on woven
cotton, applied mill-work trim
Private collection

Annie Stoltzfus married Jacob Glick
in 1892. She decorated this piece
prior to their marriage, probably
about 1890. Her cross-stitch initials
were copied from a pattern that
became popular with the Amish as
early as the 1880s. However, these
large block letters appear to have
been more commonly utilized to
mark garments than to decorate bed
linens.

Amish women, reacting slowly to
current changes in embroidery
tastes, began to integrate techniques from the larger world into
their own pieces about this time. By
the end of the first decade of the
20th century, they appear to have
opted for embroidery stitches and
largely abandoned cross-stitch.

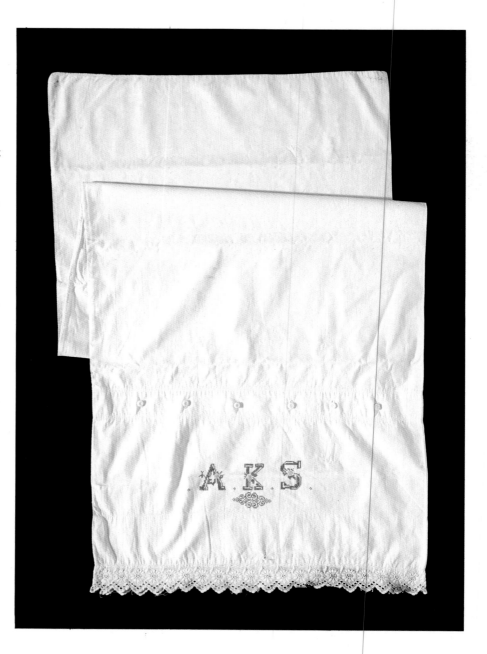

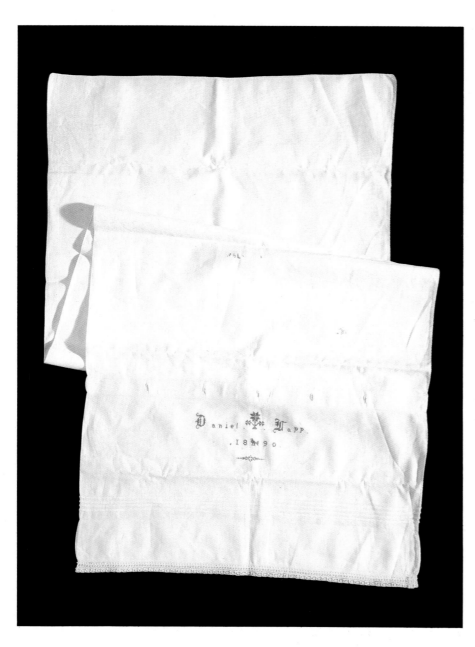

Bolster Cover
Mary Lapp
21¼ × 54
Cotton thread on woven cotton,
applied mill-woven lace trim
Kathryn and Dan McCauley

Mary Lapp (1843–1922) made this
bolster cover for her son Daniel to
take from home when he married.
It illustrates that the tradition of
cross-stitch remained popular
among the Lancaster Amish into
the 1890s, long after it lost its appeal to their neighbors.

As buttons became cheaper, they
replaced tape ties for closure during
the last quarter of the 19th century.
Pleats became popular decorative
accents, especially on children's
clothing, in the Amish community
about this time. Mary used them to
enhance the visual appeal
of Daniel's pillow coverings.

Bed sets were traditionally of four
pieces: two pillow cases, a bolster
and a mattress cover. Although bol-
sters were losing popularity with
most Pennsylvania Germans by the
end of the 19th century, they were
retained by many Amish women well
into the 20th century. Some families
continue to use them today.

Cape
Unattributed, circa 1910–1920
24 inches long, 94 inches around
at hem
Wool, cotton velvet
Private collection

The cape or mantle has been worn by young girls until about the age of ten, when they are allowed to adopt the shawl. The Lancaster style mantle is distinguished by a large shoulder-length collar, often trimmed in velvet. There are no shelves or armholes, making the design a bit restrictive. Evolution continues in the community. Sweaters and jackets for children are becoming increasingly popular. As a result, the mantle is becoming noticeably less apparent.

Boy's Overcoat
Unattributed, circa 1880
30½ inches long, 16½-inch waist,
13-inch sleeve
Wool, velvet collar, cotton lining
Private collection

Amish children's clothing mirrors adult styles in almost every detail. This coat for a three-year-old proportionately replicates dad's and has the two pockets and shoulder cape adopted by Amish men about 1860. The buttons seen here are allowed on coats, shirts, pants and jackets. Hooks and eyes serve as closures for vests. The cape overcoat is a formal style usually worn to church and social gatherings; today it is more often worn by ministers and appears to be less popular with the community as a whole. It does not appear to be worn by children or young adults.

94

Infant dresses were made with exaggerated skirts that could be wrapped under the baby's feet. Babies were dressed in wool gowns and socks. When taken outdoors they usually wore a cap, were wrapped in a blanket and had their faces covered. No skin was exposed. About 1940 enough homes were efficiently heated that the long dress gave way to shorter styles, and wool was replaced by cotton. In addition, storm fronts (glass windshields) began to appear on carriages, making them warmer and reducing road dust. As a result, the facial covering also became unnecessary, at least in Lancaster County.

Sarah Lapp married Levi Smoker in 1877. She made this dress for her daughter Elizabeth, born in 1895. It is customary to make a special dress for a baby to wear the first time she, or he, is taken to church. Amish boys often wear a dress until they are about two years of age.

Baby Dress
Sarah (Lapp) Smoker, 1895
31 inches long, 9½-inch waist,
6-inch sleeve
Wool, velvet, cotton lining
Private collection

Hand-Knit Socks

Socks on left and center, Sarah Esh, circa 1900; dated sock on right, unattributed
22¹/₃ × 6
Wool yarn
Kathryn and Dan McCauley; Dated socks: Anne and Tom Wentzel

During the late 1800s, knitting in the Lancaster Amish community became an art form. Fancy patterns and initials that demonstrated the needle skill of the maker became common. The dark primary colors specified by the Ordnung for dresses dominated the hand-knit products of Old Order women.

Sarah Esh was born September 17, 1872. She never married, but was well liked by nieces and nephews, several of whom were close enough to be considered surrogate children. In her 74 years she is said to have made numerous pairs of knit stockings for herself, family and friends.

The first pair above were made for a niece and are particularly noteworthy for the cherries knitted into the top borders. Only a few such pairs are known. The white toes with double blue bands are another notable decorative feature.

The striped pair have Sarah's initials. She put "wedding band" borders around the top and reinforced the heels with a second layer of yarn. Boldly colorful, these socks testify to Sarah's originality of design.

The unattributed, dated stockings document Amish participation in fancy knitting as early as 1876. The year and floral motif are knitted into the white border, not sewn or otherwise applied. Knitting was extremely popular in America during the 1850s, 1860s and 1870s. Patterns for knitting initials and dates into socks were published in women's magazines during this period. Amish women may have adapted some of these patterns to their own taste.

96

These stockings show the bright colors that entered Amish design after 1860.
The Amish bishop David Beiler wrote in 1862, lamenting this shift toward
worldliness. Socks with these fancy, multi-colored borders were referred to by
Amish women as "wedding" stockings. They illustrate the subtle ways these
people found to express their fondness for decoration. Amish dress did not
allow "fancies," so they devised borders for their stockings that showed above
their high shoes only when they raised their dresses to get in and out of carriages. While other Pennsylvania Germans also knitted stockings, the development of this pattern for the upper borders appears to be a singularly Amish
adaptation.

These especially vivid pairs of stockings have five colors in the upper borders and uses bright red in the body. The stockings are further enhanced by a
row of leaf vines. The popularity of adult woolen socks extended from about
1870 to 1920. Children's sizes endured until around 1930.

Wedding Stockings
Ebersole family, circa 1880
5 × 22 ¼
Wool
Kathryn and Dan McCauley

97

Knit Mittens

Black with red and green trim,
Fannie Stoltzfus, circa 1910; Wool;
8 ¾ inches long, 3-inch wrist
Red and black, Katie Glick, circa
1880; Wool; 10 ¾ inches long, 4-inch
wrist
Private collection

Hand-knit mittens usually were decorated more conservatively than knit stockings, probably because they were not concealed and were more subject to the dress Ordnung. Anything too fancy could be judged worldly and subject the owner to criticism and accusations of prideful behavior.

The tightly woven black pair was made with fine, small knitting needles by an accomplished woman. The striped mittens have a more open loop, the result of a larger needle. Their less defined shape is the result of a less experienced practitioner. The wrist border is reminiscent of that found on wedding stockings.

Knit Mittens and Gloves

1900–1920
Assorted sizes, 1½ × 4 to 4 × 12
Wool
The People's Place

Knit mittens were worn by adults and children of both sexes. Men's mittens sometimes had an index finger as well as a thumb. This made it easier to grip objects when doing winter chores in the barn.

Colorful striping, usually at the wrist, was the most common form of decoration. Initials have been found on mittens, but the dates, flowers and multi-colored bands encountered on knit stockings are not a feature of knit handcoverings.

Needle Case
Nancy Beiler, circa 1880
3½ × 4½
Wool and cotton

Star Pincushion
Hannah Zook, circa 1860–1880
3½ × 6¾
Wool

Scissor Rest
Nancy Beiler, circa 1880
1½ × 5½
Cotton and velvet

Sewing is both a major responsibility for Amish women and a major source of pleasure and creative expression. Tools involved in the process are thus valued and protected. During the 19th century, sewing needles and pins were expensive. Needles were usually kept in small cases. This made them easy to store and facilitated selection of the proper size to do a job.

Pincushions were stuffed with wool to retard the rusting of the surface of pins and needles. Loops were often attached to the pincushion, so that it could be hung from the wrist when hemming garments or strung from the corner post of a quilt frame.

Scissor rests were rolled across quilts when they were stretched in the quilting frame. The rest kept the point of the blades from damaging the fabric surface and at the same time made the scissors easier to pick up.

Tear Drop Pincushions
1880–1920
Approximately 2×3½;
some 1¼×2½
Private collection

Triangular teardrop pincushions were generally hung from the shelves in corner and dutch cupboards. The three solid-colored pieces with pom-pom yarn corners were made from men's suit linings by Barbara Ebersol between 1880 and 1900. She gave them as keepsakes to friends and relatives. The two red, white and blue examples and the small star pincushions were made by Barbara Zook, a neighbor of the Ebersols, at about the same time.

Ball Pincushions
1880–1920
2½ inches diameter to 6 inches
in diameter
Wool, cotton, cotton velvet
Private collection

Amish women's dresses are pinned for closure; no buttons are allowed. Because of this and their use in sewing, straight pins are objects of great importance. Keeping track of the number necessary for Amish homemaking requires ample and easy storage.

Pincushions of all sizes and shapes were designed to meet this need. Large cushions became popular because they are easy to see in dark, lamp-lit rooms. Size and color allowed pincushions to become decorations to hang from shelves or in china cabinets.

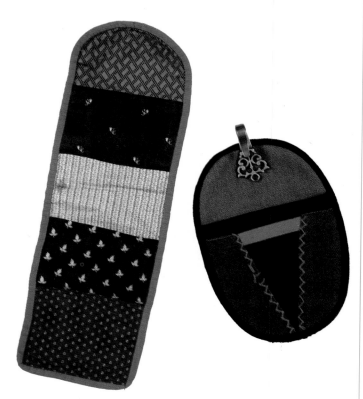

Sewing Pockets
Nancy (Stoltzfus) Beiler, 1860
4¾ × 14½; 5½ × 8
Wool, cotton
Private collection

Needle rollups and sewing pockets were used to store valued thread and needles in New England and the mid-Atlantic states from about 1780 through 1880. They held the sewing tools invaluable in households where clothing and other textiles were homemade.

Nancy (Stoltzfus) Beiler (1858–1948) used this rollup to hold her thread, thimbles and needles. It was a gift from her mother, Elizabeth (Kauffman) Stoltzfus, when Nancy began sewing during the 1860s. The oval scissor case was made about 1870. Nancy put the metal hook on her pocket to hang it from her quilting frame. The absence of patterned fabric in the scissor pocket gives it a more traditional Amish look than the calico needle rollup.

Lancaster Old Order women practiced a very broad range of textile arts, including fabric sculpture. While faceless dolls represent the most common form of Amish textile sculpture, small handsewn animal forms, particularly birds, were also popular. Two of these items—the large rooster potholder and the pincushion bird with shoe-button eyes—ostensibly have a functional purpose. However, all three pieces were actually display items for clock shelves or corner cupboards.

Fabric birds appear to have been a relatively late art form, seen among the Amish between 1870 and 1930. Inspiration may have come from the small handcarved and sometimes paint-decorated birds popular in the Pennsylvania Dutch community.

Bird Fabric Sculpture
Unattributed, 1880–1900
Small birds about 4½ × 3;
potholder 8 × 10
Wool and cotton
Wanda and Smith Johnson;
Kathryn McCauley

Pincushions

1895–1900
5×5; 7 ½×7 ½
Wool, cotton
Private collection

The red and green pincushions are initialed "BZ" for Barbara Zook and dated 1898. This design is known as the Strawberry pattern. Similar pieces and variations have been made from the 1890s up to the present.

The large needlepoint pincushion is a variation of the Sunshine and Shadow pattern. The design is executed on Berlin canvas. A backing was sewn on and the pocket stuffed with wool and sewn shut. The edge was concealed with lace, adding to the decorative appeal of the piece.

Pincushions

Circa 1880–1900
Star—6 ½×7; Crazy—6×6
Cotton, wool
Private collection

Beaded decoration was popular throughout America from as early as 1808 through World War I. Because it was perceived as a worldly art form, it was not widely adopted by Amish women. This beaded pincushion is an exception. Made by a member of the Zook family, the design is comprised of an eight-pointed star surrounded with white glass beads that make the design shimmer.

The large crazy-patch pincushion was made by Barbara Zook about 1890. The piecework is enhanced by an embroidery stitch that conceals the pieced joints. The edge is covered by a blue and white twisted cord. Large pincushions were not used to hold needles or pins but to hang from shelves or sit in the top of sewing baskets as decorations.

Pincushions

Susie Riehl, circa 1915–1925
5 ³/₄ × 5 ³/₄
Wool, cotton
Private collection

These variations of the Strawberry pattern are trimmed with a fine hand-crocheted lace. Made by Susie Riehl about 1920, they hung from the clock shelf in her kitchen for 60 years.

Small pincushions became acceptable for hanging in china cupboards after about 1850. Larger examples began to be hung from clock shelves shortly thereafter. Decorating with pincushions remains almost universal in Lancaster Amish homes.

Needlepoint Pincushions

1900–1930
Grapes—6 ¹/₂ × 6; Flower pot—
5 ³/₄ × 5 ³/₄
Wool, cotton
Private collection

The Bunch-of-Grapes pincushion was made by Emma Esh, probably before she married in 1912. Grapes are a popular Amish folk motif and a very popular quilting pattern. These pincushions are distinguished by beaded edging.

The Pot-of-Flowers pattern is a modern rendition of one of the oldest and most popular Amish designs. Lydia Beiler made this pair of cushions before her marriage in 1915. The lace trim is hand-crocheted and home-dyed to mirror the reds in the flower needlework.

Graphics

Drawing
*Unattributed, dated 1802 and
signed "Umble"
Hand-drawn and colored on
laid paper
The Free Library of Philadelphia*

While this piece has lost its history, and its attribution to an Amish creator is only speculation, it is included here because it illustrates several key premises regarding early Amish art. When viewed against the background of early Amish documented drawings, it coincides in theme, design, color and size and bears an Amish name, Umble. It is an early rendition of the bird-and-bush theme that proliferates throughout Amish art well into the 20th century. The use of color is consistent with Amish taste up through the 1940s, and the drawing fills the entire page, just as the slightly later Christian King bird-and-bush-drawing (see page 109) does.

It also typifies one problem with early Amish art: because the Germanic cultural orientation of the Amish was strong, their early work resembles that of neighboring Pennsylvania German groups so closely that it is almost impossible to differentiate one from the other.

Umble appears to have been a relatively uncommon Germanic immigrant name. Only one Amishman with this surname is documented as coming to America. Christian Umble (1749–1821) was an orphan who journeyed with the Hans Blank family from Switzerland in 1751. He married Blank's daughter Barbara about 1780, and they had three children. It is to one of these children that this piece may have belonged.

Birth Record
Johannes Kinnig (John King), 1874
7 ¾ × 12 ⅝
Hand-drawn, lettered and colored on
wove paper
Kathryn and Dan McCauley

Births have always been important events for Amish families; however, the Amish seldom made fraktur birth records as their Germanic neighbors did. Perhaps they failed to broadly accept this tradition because they did not practice infant baptism. This is one of the few known Amish fraktur birth records. It celebrates the birth of "Susanna Petersheim, maiden S. King."

The vine border was a common feature in both drawn and stitched textile art among the Lancaster County Amish, from their earliest works through the 1940s. The "hex" type pinwheels in the corners and under the signature were common Pennsylvania Dutch designs, but were not customarily included in Old Order Amish art.

The dominance of floral design is typical of Amish works, especially after 1840. Among the Amish, traditional Germanic motifs were gradually supplanted by flowers. But traditional designs are occasionally found on Amish samplers well into the 20th century.

The artist who produced this fine work was most likely Susan Petersheim's brother John, born March 15, 1832. John married Leah Lapp on March 8, 1854. This work exhibits a well-practiced script, and the date shows he was engaged in the art well into his adult years—two hints that he took fraktur seriously.

Liebes büldlein so iemand komt und will
Begfragen, so sprüch laß mich nur lieg
Ihn guten ruh dann ich gehör
Rebeca Grols fußin Zu goff gebe
Mir viel glück und segen und bringe
Mich nach dieser zeit in die
Ewig seelig keit, Amen, Ge-
schrieben den 2 tag Febru-
Arius Anno do 1822

Pot of Flowers Fraktur
Christian Kinig (King), 1822
Hand-drawn, lettered and colored on
laid paper
Muddy Creek Farm Library

The quality of this drawing suggests Christian King was well practiced in the art of fraktur. A basic Pennsylvania German motif, the pot of flowers and perching birds are found in works by numerous artists from that cultural background. Here the flowers are well defined and the writing neat and even. It is a balanced, fully developed example of Amish fraktur drawing which fully attests to both the creativity and quality found in their early pieces.

Family tradition relates that this piece was a gift from Christian to the family of Christian Stoltzfus, whose daughter Catherine he was courting. Since it was a "worldly" gift and improper for a baptized adult to accept, it was given to Catherine's sister, Rebecca, who was six at the time. The message below the drawing states: "Dear little picture, if anyone comes to carry you away respond—let me lie in good rest because I belong to Miss Rebecca Stoltzfus—God grant much success and blessing, and after this time bring me to eternal salvation, Amen. Written the second day of February in the year 1822."

Christian King (1802-1865) married Catherine Stoltzfus about 1822. Christian became a minister in 1836 and a bishop in 1856. He is reputed to have been an important conservative leader. The information regarding the drawing was related by the Amish minister Elam Stoltzfoos, a descendant, from whom the piece was obtained.

Fraktur Birth Record
Unattributed, 1874
8 ¾ × 12 ¾
Hand-drawn, lettered and colored on
wove paper
Eve and David Wheatcroft

The composition of this birth record illustrates a transition in style that was taking place in Amish art about 1860–1870. While the borders are reminiscent of early Pennsylvania fraktur, the center is an arrangement of lettering above and below a dominant central motif, a format that became the standard for Amish bookplates about 1860.

As in much Old Order art, color is skillfully used by the artist to maximize the graphic impact of the drawing. The powerful combination of raspberry, orange and navy in the bold central flower commands attention in a way that is characteristic of Amish work. The prolific use of aqua seen here is rare in Amish fraktur, but was probably chosen to brighten the presentation.

Malinda King was born October 11, 1858, to John and Leah Lapp King. The second of seven children, she went on to marry Elias Fisher on January 25, 1877, and have eight children of her own.

Catarina Petersheim is probably Malinda's cousin, identified in the *Fisher Family History* as Kathryn B. Petersheim, born July 30, 1862, to Christian and Susanna King Petersheim.

Family Record
Unattributed, circa 1828
8 × 12½; folio, two pages
Hand-drawn, lettered and colored on
wove paper
Kathryn and Dan McCauley

The distelfink, or goldfinch, was a common decorative subject for the Pennsylvania Germans and appears to have been popular among the Amish. Presented here is one of the earliest renditions by an Amish artist.

The birth dates of Barbara (June 24, 1824) and Susan King (May 18, 1826) are presented on the front beneath the distelfinks. The composition is organized within a "tombstone"-shaped border. The red and yellow in this border are used to highlight the inked lettering.

The drawn page is actually the cover of a folio, made by folding a large piece of paper in half. Inside the cover on page two are the birth dates and names of nine other children, the family of Christian and Catherine Stoltzfus King, who married about 1822. Christian was ordained a minister in 1836 and bishop in 1856, but no notation of these events is recorded on the fraktur. It is solely a family birth record.

While births and family genealogy are the subjects of fraktur among the Amish, neither baptisms, marriages, ordinations nor other noteworthy life experiences appears to have been treated with such notation.

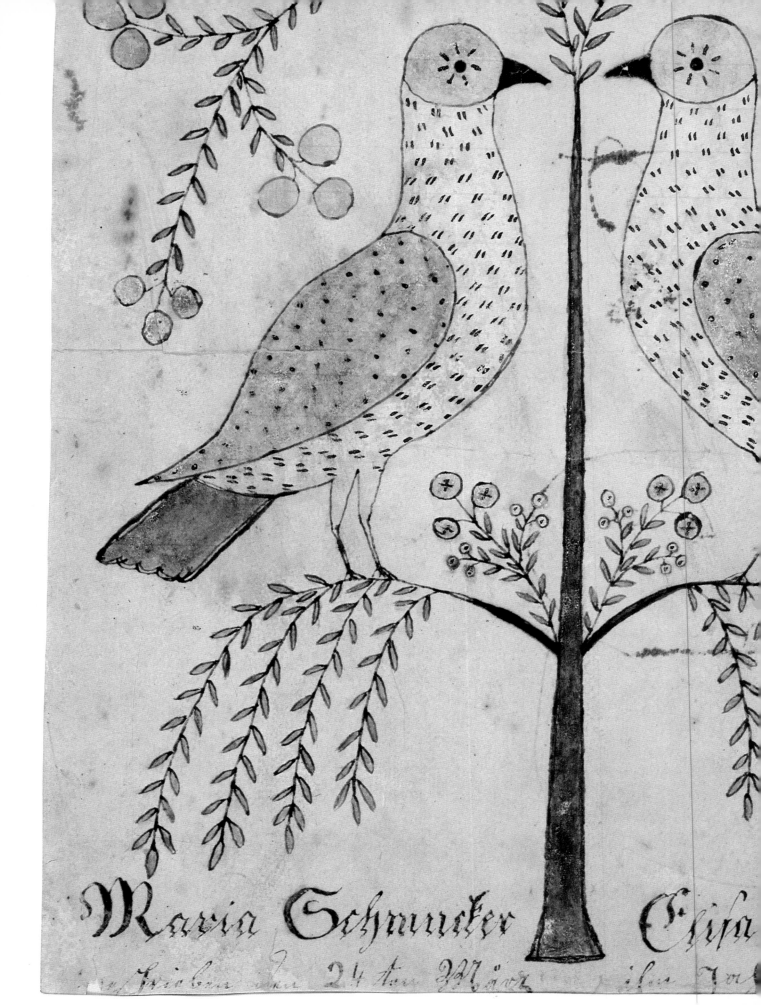

Maria Schmucker Elisa

Double Birds Drawing
Unattributed, dated 1844
Hand-drawn, lettered and colored on wove paper
Pennsylvania Farm Museum of Landis Valley

This drawing is related to several works done by Amish artists during the second half of the 19th century. Although the creator of this fraktur remains unidentified, the names "Maria Schmucker" and "Elizabeth Beiler" suggest an Amish provenance. Like other early Amish pieces the entire paper is filled by the design. The birds are large, dominating the presentation, and are substantially out of proportion to the bush.

The bird-in-bush theme runs throughout Amish graphic and textile art from the early 19th through the mid-20th century. This particular piece is similar in composition to drawings done by the Lancaster County fraktur artist David Herr about the 1830s and may be rooted in his work. It is similar to the Rebecca (Lantz) Lapp needlework in the textile section of this book (see page 37) and a drawing attributed to one of her children, either Henry or Lizzie (see page 124), as well as a dove drawing attributed to Barbara Ebersol (page 118).

An evolution of this bird and bush pattern can be seen beginning with the Umble 1802 piece with all its activity (page 106) to the Christian King piece of 1822 (page 109) to this rendition, done in 1844. One sees the syntheses of these earlier works in the later pieces of Rebecca Lapp in 1863, of her son Henry in 1880 and of Barbara Ebersol in 1860.

113

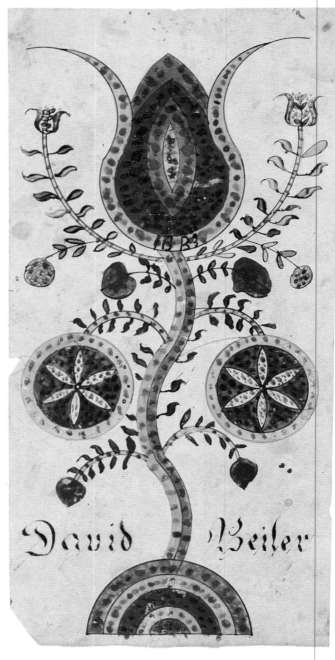

Tulip Drawing
Benjamin Beiler, circa 1845
3 ¾ × 7 ¾
Hand-drawn, lettered and colored on
wove paper
Private collection

The most ornate known fraktur to emerge from Benjamin Beiler's hand, this tulip drawing was created for his father David in 1845. Found in the family Bible, it may have been intended as a bookmark for Bishop David to mark significant passages.

Consistent with Benjamin's other works, this piece shows a craftsman's use of muted color, highlighted by a soft yellow that lightens the image and dramatizes the overall impact of the design. The ornate tulip and base document Beiler's preference for multiple decorative borders, which he modified in this case to serve as the flower stem. The pinwheel tulip buds appear to resemble the traditional Pennsylvania German "hex" signs, which were not used by the Amish and are consequently rare in their art. All in all, his graceful lines and expert use of hues result in one of the most magnificent samples of Amish fraktur found to date.

This piece is signed on the back, "Benjamin Beiler—Painter," and is initialed "BB" in the bowl of the large tulip bloom. The addition of the word "Painter" after his name indicates a vocation and that he had an acute interest in his art.

114

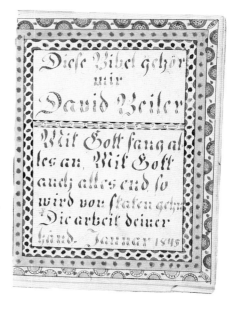

The flyleaf of the Beiler family Bible bears the notation in German: "This Bible belongs to me, David Beyler and I have received it from my father for $6 inscribed the 3rd of May 1811." Thirty-four years later, David's son Benjamin prepared this bookplate for his father's testament. The message states: "This Bible belongs to David Beiler" and is followed by a religious poem: "With God all begins, With God all ends, So will the work of your hands, Pass from this place."

David Beiler was regarded as the preeminent conservative Amish leader of his time. His conservative influence may be seen in his son's style. Here Benjamin's work appears understated when compared to most recognized Pennsylvania German fraktur artists. Despite that, a skillful use of color and simple geometric patterning are hallmarks of his style. A penchant for multiple, usually triple, borders appears to be unique in fraktur art, showing Benjamin's creativity.[14] Several similar bookplates have been discovered, all in the same format.

The combination of oak and other designs to signify tulip leaves is a feature of interest on this watercolor. Signed on the reverse, "Barbara Zook, Groffs Store PO, Lancaster Co., PA.," it is claimed by surviving family members to be both her work and signature, and not just a mark of ownership.[15]

Barbara's drawings manifest Amish women's propensity to juxtapose dark basic colors, such as her maroons and blues, against brightly contrasting shades, like the yellow used here. By balancing their compositions in this way, Amish artists displayed a sophisticated sense of how to use and place color for maximum effect. The sawtooth border adds the same understanding of organization to the fraktur that one encounters in Amish quilts.

A member of the same church community as Henry and Lizzie Lapp, Barbara Ebersol, Benjamin Beiler and possibly Frene Lapp, Barbara Zook probably knew and was influenced by them. However, she appears to have been less prolific than these artists. Other drawings by Barbara are known to still be in the hands of the Old Order Amish.

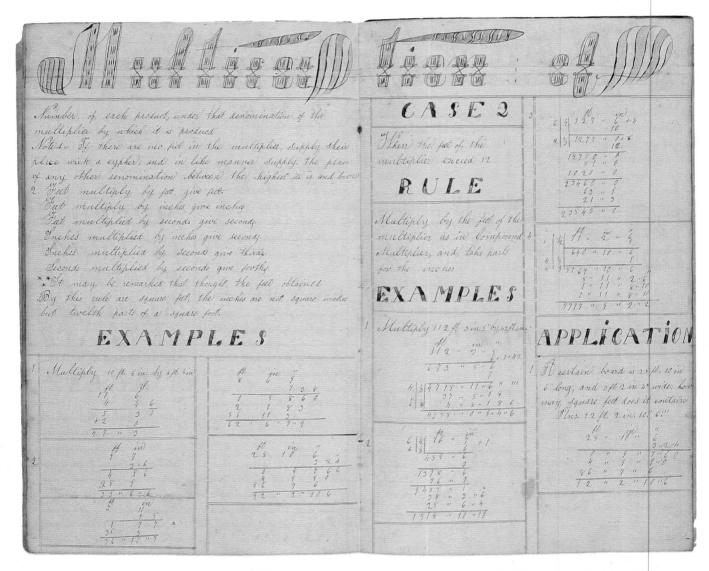

Math Book

Jonathan Stoltzfus, March 9, 1846
Hand-lettered and colored on lined
paper
Kathryn and Dan McCauley

Although rare, school notebooks done by mid-19th century Amish children have occasionally been discovered. They highlight the Amish viewpoint that, while seeking knowledge for its own sake is evidence of pride and overexposes one to the world, a basic education is valuable. Children are encouraged to obtain sufficient knowledge to run their farms and operate adequately in the world of business.

Jonathan Stoltzfus was born April 5, 1828, making him eighteen when he created this book. It appears by the sophistication of the math concepts that Jonathan was well educated. The family speculates that he may have been a schoolteacher for several years before he married; however, this has not been determined with any certainty.

The book shows a well-developed script handwriting and a typically Amish sense of color. The orange lettering is very similar in color and shape to the early works of Jonathan's niece, Barbara Ebersol, suggesting some interplay between the two.

Barbara Ebersol did this drawing for her friend Anna Stoltzfus in 1864. The compass and eight-pointed star are also found on her bookplates. The large bird in the bush is possibly a prototype for the drawing on page 118, while the potted tulip is reminiscent of the bird-in-bush theme that permeated Amish art.

Barbara chose to include a hex sign—a design commonly found in Pennsylvania German art but rarely encountered in Amish work—and a horse and rider. Mounted soldiers of a similar design are sometimes seen on Pennsylvania-Dutch decorated blanket chests. However, this is the only example to have surfaced with an Amish provenance. While the horse is well detailed and representatively presented, the face of the rider is a caricature, perhaps to conform to the church's taboo against rendering a graven, human image. The yellow and orange colors Barbara preferred before 1870 dominate this work.

Fraktur Drawing
Barbara Ebersol, 1864
11 × 14 ½
Hand-drawn, lettered and colored on wove paper
The People's Place

Dove Drawing
Attributed to Barbara Ebersol, 1869
Hand-drawn, lettered and colored on
wove paper
The Free Library of Philadelphia

The fraktur-style lettering in the name and date indicate that this drawing is the work of Barbara Ebersol. An identical piece with the name " Lea Beiler" and the date "1867" is also known, suggesting that the identity of the recipient instead of the name of the artist is recorded on these drawings.

The colors, style of the tiny leaves on the stem and varnishing of the finished painted surface are typical of Ebersol's hand and are frequently encountered on her signed bookplates.

Floral Bough Drawing

Barbara Ebersol, 1879
3 ³/₄ × 5 ⅛
Hand-drawn, lettered and colored on laid paper
Kathryn and Dan McCauley

Barbara selected a variation of her peony as the dominant motif in this drawir̲
ier Amish women and Barbara frequently adapted them to her design. She usually rendered them in two contrasting shades and often chose them as motifs for her bookplates.

The graceful sweep of this floral arrangement provides an ornamental border for Barbara's name, address and the date. The overall subtle coloration is highlighted by touches of the red Barbara seemed so fond of using. The long, gracefully contoured leaves and leaf-vine are unique among her known work.

This is her only work found to date on which she documented not only her name but her complete address. The Groff Store P.O. was originally located in the village of Mascot, but was moved to Monterey before the turn of the century. This post office serviced many of the Amish families in the Pequea congregations during Barbara's lifetime.

Crossed Flowers Drawing

Attributed to Barbara Ebersol, 1877
3 ⅛ × 4 ⅞
Hand-drawn, colored and lettered on laid paper
Private collection

Barbara Ebersol painted this small picture for her one-year-old nephew Jonas Ebersol, the son of her brother David. Here she rendered a stylized rose crossing a petunia. The large flowers on either end frame a central field that she filled with two small blooms. The curve of the stems, which is repeated in the lines of both the rose and petunia, adds a sense of lightness and grace to the drawing.

Barbara framed "*im iahr* 1877" (in the year 1877), indicating the date had significance; possibly this was a gift to Jonas on his first birthday.

Bookmark

Attributed to Barbara Ebersol, 1881
3 ⅛ × 4 ⅞
Waterpaint on wove paper
Kathryn and Dan McCauley

This drawing was found inside a small book Barbara Ebersol "marked" with a fraktur bookplate for her maternal cousin, Daniel King, in 1881. Both the drawing and bookplate have a similar "pine cone" flower motif and are executed in the same colors. However, the butterfly she used on Daniel's drawing may be unique. To date no other pieces with this motif have surfaced.

The "forget-me-not" inscription suggests that Barbara made this piece for her cousin as a remembrance. It was a common practice among the Amish to give small trinkets as keepsakes. The year, "1881," is inscribed in pencil on the reverse. The size of the drawing and the fact that it was found inside a book indicate it was intended as a bookmark.

Daniel King was born June 17, 1881. He became a deacon in 1912 and served the church in that capacity until his death in 1948. Because the Amish do not baptize infants, there is usually no special ceremony for the birth of a child. Although Barbara gave a book and bookmark to Daniel during his first six months, it is likely that they were a Christmas gift rather than a commemoration of his birth.

Bookplates
Attributed to Barbara Ebersol
Christian Blank, 3 ⅝ × 6 ⅜
Elizabeth Lantz, 3 ¾ × 6 ¾
Waterpaint on wove paper
Private collection

Christian Blank, born 1861, and Elizabeth Lantz, born 1864, married in 1883 and may have been sweethearts when these bookplates were executed. Barbara marked their books almost identically, even using the same basic flowering bush decoration. Since this was a rare motif of Barbara's, it seems more than coincidence that she chose the same for both books. It is also interesting to note that the sweep of the barber-pole borders on these two pieces is opposite. The right-to-left downward sweep on Christian's is unique; Elizabeth's represents the norm.

The barber-pole border was Barbara's favorite, but she also did a variety of leaf vines, flowering-leaf vines and straight-line borders.

Heart Bookplate
Frene Lapp, circa 1870
3¾ × 6
Waterpaint on wove paper
Kathryn and Dan McCauley

Frene Lapp's signature within the heart allows the attribution of several similar, but unsigned pieces to her hand. Common to all is the barber-pole border which she may have developed because of Barbara Ebersol's influence. The fraktur script Frene used is also similar to that of Ebersol's. While this piece is undated, several bookplates that were likely done by her date from the 1870s, along with other works from the '80s.

Frene was the second of four children born to Samuel and Anna (Stoltzfus) Lapp. Born March 10, 1843, she never married. That allowed her the time to produce the fraktur bookplates, songs and poems, notebooks and drawings she is known to have made. It appears that most Amish artists, especially the most adventurous and prolific ones, were unmarried. Perhaps since these people were not raising families there was less pressure placed upon them to conform, allowing more latitude in creative expression.

Crossed Flowers Bookplate
Attributed to Frene Lapp, 1874
4¼ × 7¼
Hand-lettered, drawn, colored on
wove paper
Muddy Creek Farm Library

Although this bookplate is unsigned, its composition, border and lettering suggest this to be the work of Frene Lapp. According to presently known pieces, she appears to have signed fewer than half of her bookplates.

The motif Frene employed here is a peony crossing a forget-me-not and is reminiscent of Barbara Ebersol's work. Frene appears to have started decorating books during the 1870s, some years after Barbara. The similarities in their work imply that Frene was strongly influenced by Ebersol.

The bookplate identifies John P. Zook as its owner. Zook was born August 21, 1855, and married Rachel Detweiler in 1878. Both John and his father, Jonathan, are believed to have been part of the "Church" group during the Great Schism of 1878–1879. The Fisher genealogy lists them as Amish-Mennonites—members of a more liberal Amish group.

**Clark's Cleveland Almanac—
1874 Drawing**
Henry Lapp, 1874
5¼ × 8
Waterpaint on wove paper
Kathryn and Dan McCauley

Henry Lapp was fond of reproducing advertising pieces, labels and magazine covers, as well as rendering small drawings of fruit, vegetables, flowers, animals and, occasionally, human subjects. His style was interpretive in terms of hue. While his subjects were realistically represented in form, they were unusually colored. Bright green goats, glowing red horses with neon blue manes, and luminous yellow squirrels were his trademark.

Here Henry improved the appeal of a basically uninteresting almanac cover by giving his animal a wonderful, whimsically naive character. Henry has accentuated the mane and chosen the unusual colors of grey and black for the lion's body. His choice of mustard and green for the nose and eyes allows them to stand out. The bold stance of the lion is enhanced by the use of red for the ground. Henry gave his lion's face a very human quality which increases its appeal, and the result is one of his best animal drawings.

This is one of a considerable number of drawings to have descended through the family of Henry's sister Sarah. At least forty drawings are known to have been handed down through her family. Based upon the number of Lapp drawings in the hands of collectors, institutions and Amish families, it appears that Henry was prolific and executed several hundred pieces.

FARMERS AND LOOK TO YUR INTEREST !

BRAMPTON, JR

Horse, Cart and Rider Drawing
Attributed to Henry Lapp, circa 1880
16 × 13
Hand-drawn, lettered and colored on wove paper
Private collection

Advertisements, promotional themes and mottoes must have fascinated Henry Lapp; he frequently copied them or used them to inspire his paintings. This example is unusually large, and has a human subject.

Lapp is known to have done a number of works depicting people.[16] Their facial features are caricatured, which may be related to the Amish taboo against replication of the human image.

Lapp worked in gum medium pigments, watercolor wash, ink and pencil. His use of bold colors infused life and interest into ordinary subjects.

Lead Glass Pitcher Drawing
Henry Lapp, 1876
5⅞ × 8⅞
Hand-drawn, lettered and colored on wove paper
Private collection

HENRY. LAPP. 1876. 27.
Lead Glass Sold by

A particularly bold and colorful drawing, this piece documents Henry Lapp's unusual color sense. He successfully blended yellow, orange and red into the body of the pitcher against the bright blue in its base and the white paper. Lapp commonly used bright strong color to decorate both his drawings and his furniture. Henry often did several renditions of the same theme in different colors, perhaps to see how color affected the image. Another version of this piece, dominated by softer yellow hues, is known.[17] Henry Lapp is believed to have executed at least 100 watercolors, probably more.[18]

123

Double Parrots Drawing
Attributed to Henry or Elizabeth
Lapp, 1875
8 × 10
Waterpaint on wove paper
Kathryn and Dan McCauley

Parrots were a popular subject with Pennsylvania German artists throughout Pennsylvania, Maryland and northern Virginia.[19] The acceptance of these and similar "Dutch" decorative motifs indicates the Amish were exposed to and influenced by the work of mainstream Pennsylvania German artists, probably seen in the homes of their non-Amish neighbors, at auctions and farm sales, and during other social occasions with outsiders.

Although unsigned, this piece descended through the family of Henry and Elizabeth Lapp from their sister Sarah to her son Daniel Lapp. A companion piece, almost identical except for the use of red for the birds and having the name, "Lizzie," penciled on the back, accompanied this drawing at one time. It can not be ascertained with certainty if Lizzie drew these pieces or was given them by Henry. It does appear that some works attributed to Henry may have been done by a different hand. Since a number of these pieces are either penciled "Lizzie" on the back or stamped "Lizzie Lapp" or "Elizabeth Lapp," it is thought that these pieces were likely her work.[20]

A number of these double parrot drawings, varying in color or detail, are known to exist. They appear to be a copy of a needlework picture stitched by the Lapp's mother, Rebecca, in 1867.

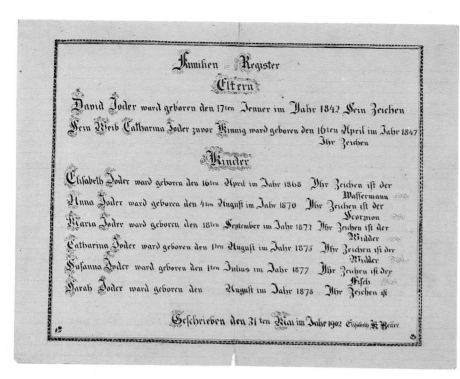

Family Record
Elizabeth K. Beiler, 1902
12½ × 15½
Ink on lined paper
Private collection

Calligraphy was done for Amish families by both their own and "English" artists from about 1885 to 1940. Decorative writing was popular for bookplates, family records and the recording of births and deaths in the family Bible. Here it is presented on a family record.

The capital letters of each family member's name are highlighted by floral decoration. An interesting feature of this piece is the inclusion of the astrological signs of most of the family members. However, the mother's and last daughter's signs are omitted.

The artist's signature and the date are enhanced by the use of multiple colors in an undisguised attempt to make them stand out, a curiously bold statement on the part of an Amish artist.

This piece was possibly made by the first child listed here, Elizabeth Yoder, who married John Beiler in 1888. The middle initial "K" would have come from her mother's maiden name, a custom commonly practiced among the Amish. Since the record is dated 1902, she would have signed her married name, Elizabeth K. Beiler.

Bookplate
Attributed to Elizabeth K. Beiler,
1897
4½ × 7
Hand-lettered, drawn and colored on
wove paper
Muddy Creek Farm Library

Several of the capital letters on this bookplate are identical in design to those on the signed Elizabeth K. Beiler family record shown on page 125. Done for Nancy K. Stoltzfus in 1897, the work is rendered in a style that was popular from about 1890 into the 1930s. Although these designs were made by both Amish and non-Amish artists, it is the decoration inside the capital letters on this example that allows an attribution to Lizzie Beiler's hand.

Elizabeth was the first child of David and Catherine (King) Yoder. She was born April 16, 1868, and married John Beiler on December 20, 1888. A number of bookplates probably decorated by her have been discovered, indicating she may have been fairly productive. Nancy K. Stoltzfus does not appear to have been a direct family relation of Lizzie's, suggesting she made pieces for more than just a few family members.

Family Record

of

Elias M. and Milinda His

Father was born January the 20 18

Mother was born October the 11 1858

John was born January the 30 1878

Aaron was born January the 28 1879

Sarah was born April the 3 1881

Ariana was born July the 14 1884

Family Record
Benjamin L. Stoltzfus, 1910
19½ × 23½, including original frame
Hand-lettered, drawn and colored on wove paper; applied floral decoration and glitter
Kathryn and Dan McCauley

Ariana Fisher ordered this family record from Benjamin Stoltzfus as a gift for her parents in 1910. It is the only fully signed example of his work yet to surface and is typical of other pieces known to be by his hand. He produced a number of family records in this format for family and friends from approximately 1905 to 1918. He abruptly discontinued his work about eight years after his marriage to Lydia Stoltzfus. It would seem that the demands of farming and family life forced him to put aside his artistic endeavors, and the demands of the ministry probably kept him from taking it up again later in life.

Works utilizing this "ribbon-candy" border design were popular in the Lancaster Amish community just after the turn of the 20th century. Several different men made bookplates with variants of this border, but it appears that only Ben Stoltzfus and Benjamin Blank (see page 129) were prolific.

Family Record
David C. Hoke, 1928
19 1/2 × 25 3/4, including original frame
Hand-lettered, drawn and colored on wove paper
Muddy Creek Farm Library

A particularly ornate family record, this piece is signed, "Made by David C. Hoke, Quentin, Pa. May 26, 1928." Quentin is in Lebanon County, which borders Lancaster to the north. Hoke drew bookplates, marked Bibles and made family records for the Lancaster Amish during the first third of the 20th century. Many still remember him as a hobo who went from farm to farm marking books for a meal and place to sleep.

Although not Amish drawn, this piece is included because it shows the style preferred by the Old Order during the early 20th century. Hoke molded his work to express Amish values. Here we see the wheat sheaves and floral designs reminiscent of works by the Amish artists Benjamin Stoltzfus and Benjamin Blank. Hoke used colors that would appeal to Old Order people and surrounded his work in subdued handmade frames that could be acceptably displayed.

This piece was made for John N. Beiler, who married Fannie Renno on December 3, 1891. Both their names and birthdates, as well as those of all their children, are noted. Family tradition relates that this piece was made by Hoke for one of the children who had married. A duplicate record tracing the spouse's genealogy is reputed to have been made at the same time. They hung together for more than fifty years, until separated at an estate sale.

128

Family Record
Benjamin Blank, 1908
19½ × 23½
Hand-lettered, drawn and colored on cardboard
Muddy Creek Farm Library

Benjamin L. Blank made this gene-alogy of the Jonas Martin family at the request of the Martins' daughter Mary. This piece is so similar in composition to pieces made by the Amish artist Benjamin L. Stoltzfus that one of the men must have copied the other. Which of the two originated the decoration is undetermined, but Stoltzfus appears to have been significantly more prolific.

Jonas Martin was an Old Order Mennonite bishop. Ordained in 1875, he sparked a revival of con-servative spirit and led a faction of his people back to the "old ways." The horse and buggy Mennonite groups seen today trace their roots to him.

Family records do not appear to have the same popularity among the Mennonites as they do among the Amish. It is interesting that one of the most conservative Mennonite leaders introduced a new art form into his community.

Taufschein
G.S. Peters Co., Harrisburg, circa 1840
17¼ × 20¼
Hand-lettered and colored on commercial form, wove paper
Private collection

Printed birth and baptismal certificates were common in southeastern Penn-sylvania during the middle of the 19th century. Records such as this were pop-ular among many of the mainstream groups who practiced infant baptism, but were rarely used by the Amish, who espoused adult baptism.

Owned by John Stoltzfus, who married Catarina Hooyinn (Catherine Hooley), this piece reports the birth of a daughter on June 20, 1827, and her baptism on "the 17th day of September, 1845." Notice the eighteen year spread between the two events, indicative of an adult ceremony. Also noteworthy is the omission of the minister who performed the service—probably an expres-sion of the Amish principle of modesty.

"Tennessee" John Stoltzfus, whose family is the subject of the record, was a nationally recognized leader of the more liberal group within the Amish church.

Furniture and
Household Objects

Sewing Box
Attributed to Henry Lapp, circa 1885–1895
7½ × 4¼ × 6⅛
Pine
The People's Place

Although no sewing boxes are pictured in Lapp's catalog notebook *A Craftsman's Handbook, Henry Lapp* (Beatrice B. Garvan, Philadelphia Museum of Art, 1975), this piece is conceptually derived from both the salt box pictured in plate #9, bottom left, and his small walnut button boxes. The red paint, yellow grained drawer and white ceramic knob are accepted hallmarks of his work, as is the robin's-egg blue interior.

Spools of thread were kept under the lid, needles and thimbles in the drawer. The box was purchased from an Amish family, but its history of ownership has been lost.

A true and accomplished craftsman, Henry Lapp provided his community with a broad range of products. Furniture, toys, household implements and containers were all made in his shop. He also sold hardware and mixed paint. Although only active for about twenty years (1885–1904) it appears that he was the most prolific Amish cabinetmaker in Lancaster County.

Seed Drawer
Henry Lapp, 1885
8 ³/₁₆ × 12 × 4¹/₄
Pine
The People's Place

The family vegetable plot was a primary responsibility of the Amish woman, so seeds were an important commodity to protect and organize. This seed box is one of several illustrated in Henry Lapp's catalog.[21]

The red paint and yellow drawers with white ceramic knobs are typical of Lapp's design. The drawers have lipped edges and are nailed together. The back is inscribed in pencil, "Sarah Lapp/Susie Ebersol 1885." The Lapps and Ebersols were members of the Pequea church district and lived in the Groff Store P.O. area. Susie may have been the daughter of David Ebersol (Susanna, born 1885).

Henry made his seed boxes to either stand on a counter or hang from a small nail. He added a back and sides to the top to facilitate storage and to keep items from falling or spilling off. The back is shaped into a graceful bell curve, in the center of which he drilled the hole for wall-mounting. The side rails are scalloped and gently slope toward the front, a feature that adds grace to the piece and eliminates a boxy look. It is subtle design features like these that witness to the extra steps taken by many Amish craftsmen to render a "plain," but pleasing product.

134

A spoon box, similar to the one shown here, appears on plate 33 of *A Craftsman's Handbook, Henry Lapp* (a copy of his notebook/catalog). Sufficient numbers of this form exist to indicate that it was very popular. All are grain-painted on the sides and have Lapp's robin's-egg blue interior. The use of pine in the construction is consistent with the other small household articles attributed to Henry Lapp.

Spoon boxes were popular because many Amish have large families. Considerable amounts of silverware are needed for meals. The spoon box could be stored in a drawer, then easily carried to the table, facilitating the chore of setting the table.

Owned by Malinda (King) Fisher, it was inherited by her namesake granddaughter in 1939. It is an Amish custom to bequeath an item to a child named after an adult. Such a gift, consequently, is known as a "namesake."

Spoon Box
Attributed to Henry Lapp, circa 1885
9 × 12 1/8 × 4 7/8
Pine
Private collection

Rocking Chair

Unattributed, circa 1840–1870
24 × 39 ¾ × 34
Mixed woods
Private collection

This rocking chair is a companion to the plank seat chair on the facing page. The painted decoration splat and the crest are identical, indicating that the rocker was part of the set. Because the shape of the splat resembles a boot-jack, this style is referred to as a "bootjack" chair. This design was very popular with the Amish and examples in this pattern were made into the 20th century, long after it was abandoned by neighboring Pennsylvania German groups.

Oversized rockers such as this were popular because they were ample enough to comfortably accommodate both mother and child. Usually purchased by young women about to start a family, these chairs accompanied them throughout their lives. Used initially for nursing they remained serviceable for the owner's entire life, into the years when they became a place to pass the time knitting or sewing.

Plank Seat Chairs
Unattributed, circa 1880
17 × 32 ¼ × 14 ¼
Poplar
Private collection

Plank seat chairs were popular throughout Lancaster County during the early part of the 19th century but declined in favor by the third quarter. This style chair found particular favor among the Amish and a set was found in almost every Amish home. (A modern version with a more stylized painted decoration is still purchased by many young married couples as they start housekeeping.)

This is one of a set of six chairs purchased by John and Susan Glick for their daughter Mary, who married Amos King in 1927. The set had descended through the family, probably from Mary's maternal grandmother, Leah (Renno) Glick. John took the chairs to the Ebersol brothers, who were starting a furniture and chair shop, to have the decoration renewed before giving them to his daughter.

Drop Leaf Table
Attributed to Henry Lapp, circa 1895
46 × 25 1/4 × 62 1/32, extended
Cherry with white pine as the secondary wood
Private collection

Gate-leg tables of similar design and structure were common throughout eastern Pennsylvania during the mid- to late 19th century. This piece compares favorably to one pictured in Lapp's catalog, including the orange-red over-paint. Red is a color that Lapp seems to have adopted as a trademark, and it appears to have found favor with the members of his community.

The table frame is marked in pencil with a "3" and a "4L." The underside of the top center panel is marked in pencil with a "4" and what appears to be "table." The legs are 6¾ inches in circumference and are distinguished by three ample ring turnings at the top. While this is a decorative feature often encountered on this style of table, these turnings are particularly bold. There is an additional ring turning where the leg narrows just above the ball feet.

It is believed Henry Lapp made this table for the Amish bishop Stephen Esh about the time of Esh's wedding to Sallie Fisher, November 26, 1896. Upon Sallie's death in 1941, it passed to their daughter Emma.

Corner Cupboard
Attributed to Henry Lapp, circa 1890
48 ¾ × 85 ¼
Pine, paint-decorated
The People's Place

Early Amish corner cupboards seem to be a rarer form than wall or "Dutch" cupboards. Although almost a 20th-century piece, this example has a number of design features carried down from earlier styles. The glass doors are cut in a tombstone shape first seen on the solid-door, 18th-century Pennsylvania cupboards made during the Queen Anne period. The turned foot, seen on most Lapp furniture, was generally popular about 1840–1860. Grain-painting was commonly done in Pennsylvania, but had fallen into disfavor in most other communities by this time. In this case, a coat of varnish was applied to protect the painted decoration, probably when the cabinet was made. Over the years this varnish has darkened and now hides the figuring in the painted surface.

The waist molding seen on many of Lapp's blanket chests has been used to improve the design and eye appeal. The cabinet is one piece rather than two, but the use of the molding suggests two pieces and gives the cupboard a more diminutive look. The interior is painted the same blue seen on many Lapp pieces.

Tall Chest
Unattributed, circa 1840
Poplar
The People's Place, Intercourse, Pa.

The tall chest was a popular furniture form among the Pennsylvania Germans as early as the mid-18th century. Amish cabinet makers continued to produce them into the 20th century. This chest, which descended through the King family, is consistent in design with other pieces from the community. The three small and four larger graduated drawers are all dovetailed and have extended edges that overlap the front. The case sits on four blunt-end turned feet and the sides are paneled as is typical of Amish cabinetwork. An unusual decorative column has been planed down the front edges. The sweeping cornice is also an uncommon aspect of this chest.

The blunt feet, moving to graduated drawers and a large, outwardly sweeping cornice, results in a graceful upward movement that disguises the overall size and shape of the piece. Admonished by the ministry early in the 19th century to make only furniture of plain design, Amish cabinet makers used subtle techniques to reduce the boxiness of larger pieces.

140

Wall Cupboard
Noah Zook, 1912
53½ × 82½
Oak, poplar as secondary wood
McCauley Law Offices

This cupboard is almost identical in style and construction to pieces known to have been made by Henry Lapp. It would seem, based upon the similarity of their patterns, that these two men were friends and that Zook may have worked or trained in Lapp's shop. After Henry's death, Zook set up his own business in Intercourse, just down the road from Henry Lapp's old shop in Bird-in-Hand.

Zook made this cupboard for Betsy Stoltzfus about the time she married Aaron Beiler. It is signed on the back of the upper case, "made by Noah Zook, Intercourse, 1912." The inside is painted blue like Lapp's cupboards, but the door panels have a more exaggerated oval curve, an attempt at modernizing the design.

Zook carefully selected the oak he used in this piece to maximize the visual impact of the wood's grain. Oak began to replace walnut as the wood of choice among the Lancaster Amish during the early 20th century. Unfortunately, it appears that at this time many of the old red and blue painted pieces were over-grained in yellow to look like oak, an attempt by Amish women to make inherited furniture look more modern.

Blanket Chest
Attributed to Henry Lapp, 1900
48 ⅜ × 26 ⅝ × 22 ⅞
Poplar, pine
Kathryn and Dan McCauley

Henry Lapp appears to have made blanket chests in a variety of sizes. Drawers in the bottom of the case or painted decoration were optional. In this example the top overhangs the case and has applied molding around the front and side edges, forming a lip.

Henry painted the drawers in an imitation oak pattern. He deliberately accentuated the graining to resemble a wood knot moving from the center outward. The work is so realistic that the finished product looks like a natural surface.

Above the drawers is a molding painted yellow. This molding is seen on many of Lapp's blanket chests, Dutch cupboards, corner cupboards and other pieces. The box sits on four turned feet, similar in design and style to those on other pieces attributed to his shop.

The chest is painted a reddish-orange with the owner's initials, a compass star and the year the chest was made done in black. A bird and butterflies are decals, not painted figures. Decal decoration was popular among the Amish at the turn of the century.

Jelly Cupboard
Unattributed, circa 1840
49 ³⁄₄ × 59 ¹⁄₂ × 18
Poplar with pine shelves
Private collection

Cupboards of this design were so versatile that they were used to store fruits and preserves in the kitchen or clothing and linens in the bedroom. Known as a jelly cupboard because of its kitchen service, one was usually found in a Pennsylvania German farmhouse.

This cupboard descended through the Stoltzfus family and is representative of mid-19th century Lancaster Amish design. It compares favorably to one illustrated in Henry Lapp's *Craftsman's Handbook*, plate 7, but this one is of superior design.[22]

The three-sided gallery top is shaped and gradually descends in height from back to front, thus improving its eye appeal. The doors are paneled in four panes as opposed to two, and there are three drawers rather than Lapp's two. The feet are taller than those found on later pieces. The chamfered outside edges, the white knobs and the red finish are typical Amish design features. The top has a unique applied, updrafting lip to keep items from rolling off the front.

The size of the piece is skillfully camouflaged by the small panels, use of three smaller drawers, descending gallery and chamfering of the outside edges. Several such well-composed pieces possibly originating from a single shop are known.

Miniature Dutch Cupboard
David Flaud, 1910–1920
24 × 38 ¾ × 12 ¾
Pine, grain-painted
Private collection

David Flaud, a carpenter by trade, was married to Fannie Beiler, a niece of Henry Lapp. Flaud may have fashioned this chest in Henry's abandoned workshop, which was used occasionally by family members until it was torn down in the mid-20th century.[23]

David made a miniature version of a cupboard found in most Amish kitchens and known as a "combine." The name is probably a reference to the origin of the design. The base was a dry sink combined with an overhead cupboard. As indoor plumbing replaced buckets from the well, the dry-sink gallery was removed to permit storage on a flat surface.

More than a toy, this cupboard is a well conceived replica of a full-size design. The upper and lower doors are paneled. There is a cornice molding below the top. The feet are clearly defined and cut out along the base, and the cabinet's side supports are cut in a delicate reverse "S" curve that adds to an overall sense of grace and symmetry.

The white porcelain knobs were popular among the Amish until about 1930. The front and sides of the piece are grain-painted to resemble oak, which began to replace walnut in popularity about 1890.

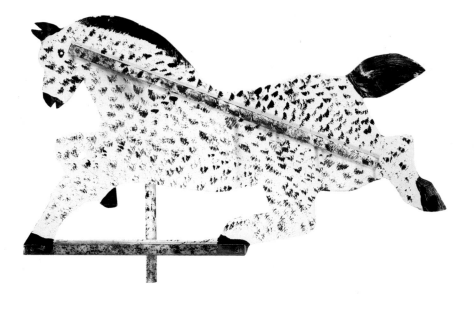

Running Horse Weathervane
Abraham King, circa 1940
23½ × 36½
*Hand-decorated sheet metal, iron
bracing and pipe*
Private collection

Sheet-metal weathervanes have long
been popular among the Amish.
They decorate barns and carriage
sheds throughout Lancaster County.
This example was probably copied
from the more expensive three-
dimensional commercial vanes that
reached the height of popularity in
this country during the second half
of the 19th century.

Many of those used by the Amish
are reputed to be homemade, while
others may possibly have been cut
by one or two unidentified artists.
As with other Amish crafts, the patterns and designs were shared. Animal subjects, particularly horses,
were the principal designs.

Abraham King painted this vane
and placed it atop his carriage barn
about 1940. Most Amish vanes are
silhouettes and are simply painted
black to protect them from the ele-
ments. Many have some white detail
highlighting to help them stand out
on dark days. Abraham chose to
paint his off-white and dapple it
with black brush strokes. In so
doing he enlivened the design and
gave his horse character, elevating it
above a common sheet-metal
silhouette.

Toy Train
Levi Esh, circa 1930
2¾ × 3¾ × 18 overall length
Oak
Private collection

This toy is a silhouette of the train that passed through Gordonville, Lancaster
County, during the 1920s and '30s. Levi Esh took this purely "English" vehicle and transformed it to conform to the Amish value of simplicity—a hall-
mark of Old Order craft.

The conventional black engine and coal cars are enhanced by the use of
orange, a color that appealed to the Amish eye. Wheels were left out, likely
because the oak would resist wear and because they were not necessary to the
concept of a train. Without them the idea of a train is reduced to its essence.

Levi Esh married Annie Smoker in 1885. Identified in the *Fisher Family
History* as a carpenter, he fashioned at least five identical train sets out of
hardwood flooring for his young sons and their friends.

Basket

Unattributed, circa 1910–1925
12 × 7 × 8½
Bamboo, ash splint, copper hinge,
painted decoration
Private collection

Known simply as a "Kavli," baskets of this design have been made by the Lancaster Amish for generations. Although they look like sewing baskets and do serve as such, they were (and still are) used primarily by young mothers to carry baby diapers and assorted notions to church and family gatherings. These baskets do not seem to have been popular in the midwestern communities and were used almost exclusively in Lancaster.

Mastering all the weaves required to produce a kavli demanded substantial practice. The red, green and black paint was applied to the components before weaving began. The splint used to attach these decorative features was also painted in advance. The handles and lid were fastened to the body by loops of copper wire.

This basket was owned by Susie Riehl, who lived in the village of Intercourse, Lancaster County. She is known to have carried it throughout her lifetime. It was purchased several years ago from her estate.

Henry Lapp made two designs of small walnut boxes in graduated sizes. His smaller boxes, from 4¾ inches × 2¼ inches up to at least 8 5/16 inches × 4 3/16 inches, were popularly used as button boxes. The larger sizes, 11¼ inches × 4½ inches, tended to be shallower—2¼ inches as opposed to 3 inches—and were used to store candles, lamp wicks, matches and pencils. The medium-size button boxes appear to have been the more popular.

Henry often presented small boxes to friends and family as tokens of his affection on birthdays and weddings. Occasionally a dedication is found inside the lid or on the bottom.

On these examples the four sides and tops are walnut; the bottoms are pine. The hinges on the button boxes are tacked to the tops and screwed to the bottoms. For hinging the candle boxes he used only screws. As decoration, Henry often applied decals to the fronts or tops of the boxes, finishing them with a coat of varnish.

The box bearing the initials "E.L." was given by Henry to his sister Lizzie in 1904 and is dated on the top. The box with the decal of the Chinese men on the lid was Henry's own. Both pieces were passed to a niece upon Lizzie's death.[24]

Button and Candle Boxes
Henry Lapp
4¾ × 2¼ × 11½ × 4¾
Walnut and pine
Kathryn and Dan McCauley

Button Box
Box by Henry Lapp, circa 1880
Decorated by Mary Lapp, 1930
4 1/8 × 2 3/4
Hand-decorated, handmade
walnut box
Private collection

Sewing is one of the Amish woman's fundamental responsibilities. Since most clothing has been homemade, tools to accomplish this are valued by Amish wives and mothers. Mary Lapp probably had this in mind when she chose a button box, made by her relative Henry Lapp fifty years earlier, to paint as a wedding gift for her friend Sallie Beiler.

The beige background is consistent with the light shades Mary favored for this purpose. The red picture-frame border is one of her hallmarks. She used the same red to border the sides and front. The grapevine motif may have been inspired by the grapevine quilting pattern popular during the 1930s.

Sallie Beiler's initials and the year 1930 are painted in black on the inside lid. Among known objects, Mary consistently used black paint for her dedications.

Decorated Miniature Blanket Chest
Mary Lapp, 1929
14 1/2 × 6 3/4 × 6 1/2
Hand-drawn, lettered and colored
Kathryn and Dan McCauley

Mary Lapp took an old wooden box, attached thread spools for feet and paint-decorated the piece as a gift for her friend Mary Glick King, who had wed Amos King in 1929. Like many of Mary Lapp's other pieces, the top has the owner's initials on either side of a pitcher. The front depicts a rose branch bordered by parrots carrying the year 1927 in their beaks. Red picture-frame borders contain Mary's designs on the front, top and two sides. The background color is a blue/green shade Mary often used as a backdrop for her decoration.

Painted Tin
Mary Lapp, 1932
5 inches square × 9½ inches tall
Oil paint over tin
Private collection

Brush Holder
Mary Lapp, 1933
3 ⅞ × 4 ⅝
Enamel paint over tin
Private collection

The dark wool clothing worn by the Amish required frequent use of a clothes brush. Many women stored their brushes in tubes, which they hung by yarn or string on hooks near their clothing.

In 1933, folk painter Mary Lapp decorated a tin can, transforming it into an attractive brush holder. She made it for her friend Barbara Ebersol, whose first name appears on the front, along with the year the gift was presented. Mary commonly dated the objects she painted and identified the owner, usually by initials.

Even more than the brush holder, the larger tin shown above testifies to Mary's careful planning, artistic color sense and patient attention to detail. Each side of this decorated coffee can has a central motif of its own, while the work is tied together by the skillful use of common upper and lower borders. Throughout the piece, subtle color highlighting is used as shading to define and add life to the motifs.

Mary's use of this color technique attests to her skill. It is an example of the academic qualities this tin has that are seldom found in the work of an unschooled artist. Completed about seven years after Mary took up the brush, this piece shows the extent of her talent.

151

Bandbox
Leah Zook Stoltzfus, 1898
8 × 11 × 6
Pasteboard, wallpaper-covered,
newspaper-lined
Private collection

Originally an 18th century English invention to store collar bands, these boxes were particularly popular in America during the second quarter of the 19th century[25]. Usually oval or circular in shape, they were valuable to farm women who lived in homes with limited built-in cabinets. Wardrobes and blanket chests were the basic storage units. Small containers and boxes were used on blanket chest and dresser tops or placed on wardrobe shelves.

Though commercially-made boxes were available, the Amish usually constructed their own. Leah Zook made the example shown here, which was inherited by her granddaughter Emma. Leah probably made this box in 1898, because it is lined with a copy of the *Sugarcreek Budget*, dated January 6 of that year. The *Budget* still serves Amish and Old Order Mennonite communities across North America.

Stored out of sight, boxes such as this one were covered with "fancy" or "worldly" patterned papers that became available with the advent of machine-roller printing. Surviving examples suggest that wallpaper boxes reached the height of their popularity among the Lancaster Amish about fifty years after peaking in "English" society.

Biographies

Benjamin Beiler

Benjamin Beiler was born April 26, 1830, the eighth and last child of Bishop David and Elizabeth Fisher Beiler. A number of fraktur pieces, mostly bookplates, are credited to him.

Benjamin's known works were made during his teenage years. One piece is signed "Benjamin Beiler—Painter," showing that he considered fraktur a vocation.

Benjamin produced two known ornate works—a tulip bookmark and a Bible bookplate—for his father, a conservative Amish leader in Pennsylvania. It is highly significant that Bishop Beiler not only condoned decorative fraktur but seems to have supported his youngest son's work in this medium.

Benjamin married Mary Esh on January 22, 1857. The couple lived on a farm in the Pequea area and had eight children. The duration of Benjamin's involvement in fraktur is unknown. He died January 6, 1910, at the age of 79, two years after the death of his wife of fifty years.

Barbara Ebersol

Barbara, known to the Amish as "Bevlie," was born May 18, 1846, to Christian and Elizabeth Stoltzfus Ebersol. She suffered from genetic dwarfism and appears to have had trouble walking.[1] Her crutches still exist.

A seamstress by trade, Barbara was also fond of decorating towels and pillow cases.[2] In addition, she made fraktur drawings, several of which have survived.

Barbara started making fraktur bookplates for family and friends as early as 1859 and worked in that art form until about 1918. Many of her signed pieces, dated 1860, have survived.

Barbara is reputed to have had an eccentric personality, yet was well liked among her people. She often visited relatives and friends for periods of a week or more. On summer evenings, she sat on her porch and frugally smoked half a cigar at a time.[3] She covered empty cigar boxes with wall paper, then gave them to children as keepsakes. Often these boxes bear initials and dates inside the lid.

Barbara never married, but lived with her brother Jacob and sisters Anna and Catherine until she died on April 17, 1922.

Among the characteristics of Barbara's fraktur work are strong lettering, composition and design. Most of her early bookplates are unsigned. They are simply decorated and have two-tone script letters. By 1870 she began to use more floral themes and adopted a bold, black script. She also began to sign her work more frequently.[4] At about the same time, she seems to have abandoned the practice of making double-page bookplates.

Barbara became less prolific after the turn of the century. Fewer of her smaller bookplates dated in the 1900s are known.

Of the many border motifs that Barbara used, the barber pole seems to have been her favorite. Vine leaves and floral vine motifs also appear frequently. In addition, Barbara made some plates with simple, straight-ruled borders. These seem to be her rarest perimeter work and are usually found on her later plates.

It appears that Barbara varnished or otherwise painted over the majority of her decorative motifs to protect them. Floral subjects were her first choice for decoration, followed by stars, hearts and geometric shapes. There are no known bookplates by her bearing bird or animal decorations.

On occasion, after marking the inside of a book, Barbara would ink the initials of the owner and a small decorative motif on the page edge of the book. These initials, in black, made it easy for owners to identify their property at church, where other copies of the same book were found.

Throughout her life, Barbara preferred strong Amish colors. She shows a particular fondness for shades of red, green and blue.

Frene Lapp

Veronica Lapp, known as "Frene," was born March 10, 1843, to Samuel and Anna Stoltzfus Lapp and grew up in the Mill Creek/ Pequea area.

Frene was a neighbor and friend of Barbara Ebersol, and appears to have undertaken fraktur about a decade after Barbara. The similarity in composition of the two women's bookplates indicates that Frene emulated her friend. While Barbara was more prolific, enough pieces by Frene's have been uncovered to show that her work was in demand.

Frene, who remained single all her life, wrote poetry and hymns in addition to making fraktur. She collected her writings in several booklets, which she meticulously lettered in fraktur script.

Little more is known about her. Outside of her artistic activity in the 1870s and 1880s, she seems to have led a typically anonymous Amish life.

Henry Lapp

Born August 18, 1862, to Michael K. and Rebecca Lantz Lapp, Henry was deaf and partially mute, probably from birth.[5] A cabinet-maker and hardware store owner by trade, he lived along the Old Philadelphia Pike (now Route 340) with his maiden sister Lizzie.[6] Henry made frequent trips to Philadelphia, where he had a market for his furniture and bought supplies for his hardware business.[7]

Henry produced a myriad of whimsical folk art drawings, featuring bird, fruit, animal, floral and a few human subjects. Many of these pieces are signed and dated—an unusual practice among the Amish because signing one's work tended to be interpreted as a sign of pride.

Henry's naive perceptions and color selections resulted in unique renderings of what he saw: red horses with blue manes and rainbow-feathered birds, for example.

To publicize his businesses, he produced his own catalog of hand-sketched and watercolored drawings, now part of the collection of the Philadelphia Museum of Art. The catalog contained graphic representations of Henry's products, including furniture, toys, storage chests of various shapes and sizes, tools, puzzles, dominoes and even a calculating machine.

As a furniture-maker, Henry appears to have favored walnut and cherry, although he would often use pine or poplar if a customer ordered a paint-decorated piece. Curiously, Henry sometimes painted his hard-wood pieces as well. His favorite color seems to have been an orange-red, though he often painted drawers yellow and the inside of cupboards a robin's egg blue. In addition, he is known to have decorated some pieces with the oak grain that became popular with the Lancaster Amish about the turn of the century.

Henry died July 5, 1904. Tradition says that he was a victim of lead poisoning, which he could have contracted from mixing the paint he sold in his store.

Leah Lapp

Leah was born May 31, 1873, to David and Rebecca Beiler Zook, and married Christian L. Lapp, an Amish minister, on December 7, 1893. She died on March 24, 1966. David and Leah had ten children, but only four survived to adulthood.

Leah was a cousin of folk painter Mary Lapp, and seems to have acquired her interest in art from Mary in the late 1920s.[8] Unlike her cousin, Leah favored strong colors as backgrounds for her painting. Her borders are thin and relatively undefined, while her flowers are large and dominate the overall design.

Lizzie Lapp

Elizabeth Lapp, known as "Lizzie" to friends and relatives, was born February 28, 1860, two years before her brother Henry. Like him, she apparently had a speech impairment, perhaps related to a genetic hearing problem.

A seamstress by trade, she marked patterns to decorate pillows, towels and rugs.[9] It is possible that some of the drawings attributed to Henry were actually done by Lizzie.[10]

Lizzie was known for the rag dolls that she made. According to family tradition, she sold these not only to the Amish but to tourists who visited her brother's shop. In addition, she appears to have sent a number of her dolls to dealers in New York and California.[11]

Lizzie died unmarried on November 19, 1932.

Mary Lapp

Mary was born October 15, 1875, to Bishop Henry and Leah Zook Stoltzfus. She married Daniel Lapp on Christmas Day, 1894.

Mary and Daniel had eleven children. As her family got older, Mary began to make fraktur bookplates and to paint small boxes with floral motifs for friends and relatives. Eventually, people began to bring her objects to decorate, from cigar boxes to chairs.

Mary was active from about 1924 to 1934, when she suddenly came to believe that painting was not a proper use of her energies. She abandoned her artwork to become a seamstress.[12]

Like all Old Order Amish folk artists, Mary was self-taught. Floral motifs dominate her work. One of her favorite rose motifs is copied from the decorated plank-seat chairs present in most Amish homes.

Most of Mary's flowers and borders are a deep red. She often contrasts these strongly colored motifs against a soft background.

Many of Mary's pieces were given as gifts. The initials or name of the recipient are commonly included in her decoration. When she signed her work, she usually did so inconspicuously by initialing a bookplate or painting a dedication inside the lid of a box.

Mary died May 7, 1955.

Benjamin L. Stoltzfus

Benjamin was born September 25, 1888, to the minister Stephen F. Stoltzfus and his wife, Susan (Lantz) Stoltzfus. On December 8, 1910, Benjamin married Lydia Stoltzfus. The couple had ten children.

Benjamin was ordained an Amish bishop in 1931. He and Lydia were one of the first Amish couples to move to St. Mary's County, Maryland, in 1941 as a result of the Amish school crisis in Lancaster County. (See page 59.) He died in Charlotte Hall, Maryland, on January 4, 1951.

Benjamin drew and decorated family records and bookplates from about 1908 to 1915. He used a multicolored peak and valley border, reminiscent of ribbon candy, surrounding a hand-lettered field.[13] His work is decorated with commercially-printed floral sprigs that he removed from calling cards popular among the Amish in the 19th century.

Noah Zook

Little is known about Noah Zook. He was born January 28, 1879, one of seven children of Eli and Mattie (Fisher) Zook, and he married Rebecca Beiler on January 4, 1900.

Noah was a cabinetmaker who knew and may have trained with Henry Lapp. Their furniture patterns are nearly identical. Noah had a shop in Intercourse as late as 1912, and he is believed to have worked for the Ebersol brothers in their chair shop before his death on February 19, 1935.[14]

Endnotes

Endnotes for The Amish and Their Decorative Culture (pages 9–25)

[1] Claude Levi-Strauss, *The Savage Mind*. Chicago: University of Chicago Press, 1969, pp. 16–22.

[2] Even though Pennsylvania did recognize persons claiming the conscientious objector position, some Amish were drafted. See Document 33 in Paton Yoder, *Tennessee John Stoltzfus: Amish Church-Related Documents and Family Letters*. Lancaster, Pennsylvania: Lancaster Mennonite Historical Society, 1987.

[3] For more on the subject of 19th century Amish decor and clothing, see excerpts from David Beiler's diary in John Umble, "Memoirs of an Amish Bishop," *Mennonite Quarterly Review* (1948), pp. 94–115.

See also Yoder, p. 176.

[4] Ellen H. Gehret and Alan Keyser, *This is the Way I Pass My Time*. Birdsboro, Pennsylvania: Pennsylvania German Society, 1985, p. 8.

[5] Judith Weissman and Wendy Lavitt, *Labors of Love: America's Textile and Needlework, 1650–1930*. New York, New York: Knopf, 1987, p. 151.

[6] Umble, pp. 94–115.

[7] A survey of notices of public sales posted in *Lancaster Farming* during 1985 and 1986 shows that most Amish sales advertise old hooked rugs to be sold. That is one manifestation of the proliferation of this art form throughout the community.

[8] Harold S. Bender, translator and editor, "Some Early American Amish Disciplines," *Mennonite Quarterly Review* (April, 1934), p. 94, Article 3.

[9] Yoder, p. 76.

The Ministers Conference of 1837 resolved that, "Cabinet-makers are not to make such proud kinds of furniture and not decorate them with such loud and gay colors," Bender, *Mennonite Quarterly Review* (April, 1934).

[10] Bender, pp. 92, 94, 96.

[11] James Nelson Gingerich, "Ordinance or Ordering: Ordnung and Amish Ministers Meetings, 1862 and 1878," *Mennonite Quarterly Review*, LX, 2 (April, 1986), p. 195.

Bender, pp. 90–98.

[12] Cornelius J. Dyck, ed., *An Introduction to Mennonite History*. Scottdale, Pennsylvania: Herald Press, 1967, pp. 40–43.

[13] John A. Hostetler, *Amish Society*. Baltimore, Maryland: Johns Hopkins University Press, 1980, p. 20.

[14] Dyck, pp. 34–35.

[15] Joseph F. Beiler, "Our Fatherland in America, The Northkill Congregation—Its Formation," *The Diary* (June, 1972), p. 120.

[16] Hugh F. Gingerich and Rachel W. Kreider, *Amish and Amish Mennonite Genealogies*. Gordonville, Pennsylvania: Pequea Publishers, 1976.

[17] Gottlieb Mittelberger (O. Handin and J. Olive, translators), "Journey to Pennsylvania," *The Diary* (January, 1979).

[18] Ibid.

[19] S. Duane Kauffman, "Miscellaneous Amish Mennonite Documents," *Pennsylvania Mennonite Heritage* (July, 1979), p. 12.

[20] Joseph F. Beiler, "A Review of the Founding of the Lancaster County Settlement Based on the Alms Book and the Ministry," *The Diary* (December, 1983), p. 18.

[21] Kauffman, pp. 15–16.

[22] Ibid., p. 13.

Joseph F. Beiler, "A Review of the Founding of the Lancaster County Settlement Based on the Alms Book and the Ministry," *The Diary* (December, 1983).

[23] Ibid.

[24] Umble, pp. 94–115.

[25] Beiler, *The Diary* (December, 1983), p. 10.

[26] Ibid., p. 19.

[27] Ibid.

[28] Ibid.

[29] Hostetler, p. 59.

"A Review of the Founding of the Lancaster Church Settlement," *The Diary* (December, 1983), pp. 17–22.

[30] Hostetler, p. 64.

[31] Joseph F. Beiler, "Our Fatherland in America, Shiplists," *The Diary* (July, 1972), p. 140.

[32] Gingerich and Kreider, p. xiii.

[33] Ibid., p. xix.

[34] Beiler, *The Diary* (July, 1972).

[35] Ibid.

[36] Conversation with historian Abner Beiler, librarian of the Pequea Bruderschaft Library, Gordonville, Pennsylvania, on December 2, 1987.

[37] For a list of church divisions, ministers and districts, see Old Order Map Committee, *Pennsylvania Amish Directory, Lancaster and Chester County Districts*, 1973.

[38] A reading of Beiler's diary reveals a reluctance on the part of some members of the ministry to accept changes in clothing. Umble, pp. 94–115.

[39] Paton Yoder, "Baptism as an Issue in the Amish Division of the Nineteenth Century: 'Tennessee' John Stoltzfus," *Mennonite Quarterly Review*, LIII (October, 1979), pp. 306–323.

[40] Ibid.

Christine Stoltzfus, *Golden Memories of Amos J. Stoltzfus*. Gordonville, Pennsylvania: Pequea Publishers, 1984, p. 136.

[41] Gingerich, *Mennonite Quarterly Review*, p. 185.

[42] Ibid., p. 180.

[43] Ibid., pp. 187, 189.

44 Old Order Map Committee. Stoltzfus, p. 136.

45 Elmer S. Yoder, p. 110.

46 Ibid.

47 Elmer S. Yoder, pp. 354–355.

Endnotes for Gallery Captions (pages 27–154)

1 Ellen J. Gehret and Alan Keyser. *The Homespun Textile Tradition of the Pennsylvania Germans*. Harrisburg, Pennsylvania: Pennsylvania Historical and Museum Commission, 1975, p. 8.

2 Ibid.

3 H. Harold Hartzler, *The King Family History*. Private publication, 1984.

4 Margaret Schiffer, *Miniature Antique Furniture*. Wynnewood, Pennsylvania: Livingston Publishers, 1972, p. 56.

5 Author's conversation with Fisher sisters, June, 1984.

6 Robert Bishop and Elizabeth Safanda, *A Gallery of Amish Quilts*. New York, New York: E. P. Dutton, 1976, plate 42.

7 Author's conversation with David and Eve Wheatcroft, Amish quilt collectors and historians.

8 Julie Silber, *Catalog of the Esprit Quilt Collection*. San Francisco, California: Esprit de Corp., 1985, plate 1.

9 Author's conversation with Emma Stoltzfus Ebersol in December, 1987, regarding the attitudes of her mother, Mamie Lapp Stoltzfus, who did a significant amount of paint decorating.

10 Author's conversation with Annie Fisher King in February, 1985, and with the Fisher sisters in June, 1984.

11 Author's conversation with Annie Stoltzfus in September, 1983, when the dolls were purchased.

12 Gehret and Keyser, p. 8.

13 Ibid.

14 A survey of published fraktur does not reveal any with border treatments close enough to Benjamin Beiler's to suggest that he copied other's work.
Howell J. Heaney and Frederick S. Weiser, *The Pennsylvania German Fraktur of the Free Library of Philadelphia*. Breinigsville, Pennsylvania: Pennsylvania German Society, 1976.
Scott T. Swank, *The Arts of the Pennsylvania Germans*. New York, New York: W. W. Norton Co., 1983, pp. 230–264.

15 Author's conversation in May, 1986, with Enos K. Zook, who identified this as his grandmother's work.

16 On display and in the collection of The People's Place, Intercourse, Pennsylvania.

17 Ibid.

18 Lestz, p. 86.

19 Francis M. Lichten, *Folk Art of Rural Pennsylvania*. New York, New York: Bonanza Books, 1946, p. 196.

20 Margaret A. Witmer, "Henry and Elizabeth Lapp, Amish Folk Artists," *Antique Collecting* (May, 1979), pp. 22–27.

21 Garvan, plate 28, items 80, 81 and 82.

22 Ibid., plate 7.

23 Author's conversation with Emanuel Flaud in 1987, when the cupboard was purchased.

24 Author's conversation with Fannie Flaud, niece of Henry Lapp, at her estate sale in 1987; history corroborated by Emmanuel Flaud, her nephew, at the same sale.

25 Mary Jean Madigan, *Americana Folk and Decorative Art*. New York, New York: Art and Antiques, 1982, pp. 126–131.

Endnotes to Biographies of Known Amish Artists (pages 155–157)

1 Gerald S. Lestz, *Amish Culture and Economy*. Ephrata, Pennsylvania: Science Press, 1984, p. 77.

2 Author's conversation with John and Sarah Ebersol, April, 1985.

3 Author's conversation with John Ebersol, April, 1985.

4 Examination by authors of more than 100 pieces of Ebersol's work.

5 Beatrice B. Garvan, *A Craftsman's Handbook, Henry Lapp*. Philadelphia, Pennsylvania: Philadelphia Museum of Art, 1975, p. 2.

6 Lestz, p. 86.

7 Garvan, pp. 2,3.

8 Author's conversation with Sarah King Lapp, September, 1986.

9 Author's conversation with Annie Lapp King, April, 1985.

10 Margaret A. Witmer, "Henry and Elizabeth Lapp, Amish Folk Artists," *Antique Collecting* (May, 1979), pp. 22–27.

11 Author's conversation with Fannie Beiler Flaud, February, 1987.

12 Author's conversation with Mary Lapp Bawell, November, 1984.

13 "Ribbon candy" description coined by David Luthy, librarian for Amish Historical Library, Aylmer, Ontario.

14 Antique cupboard pictured on page 142 of this volume is fully signed on the back, indicating that he worked in Intercourse.

Conversation with Barbara Ebersol, August, 1986.

Bibliography

Bath, Virginia Churchill. *Needlework in America*. Viking Press, New York, New York, 1979.

Beiler, Joseph. "A Review of the Founding of the Lancaster County Church Settlement Based on the Alms Books and the Ministry," *The Diary*, 1983.

Bender, Harold S. "An Amish Church Discipline of 1781," *Mennonite Quarterly Review*, IV (April, 1930), pp. 140–148.

Bender, Harold S. "Some Early Amish Mennonite Disciplines," *Mennonite Quarterly Review*, VIII (April, 1934), pp. 90–98.

Bender, Harold S. "An Amish Bishop's Conference Epistle of 1865," *Mennonite Quarterly Review*, XX (July, 1946), pp. 222–229.

Bishop, Robert and Safanda, Elizabeth. *A Gallery of Amish Quilts*. E. P. Dutton, New York, New York, 1976.

Blanke, Fritz. *Brothers in Christ*. Herald Press, Scottdale, Pennsylvania, 1961.

Butterfield, Jim. "An Amish Farm," *The Pennsylvania Dutchman*, Spring, 1957.

David, Kenneth Ronald. *Anabaptism and Asceticism*. Herald Press, Scottdale, Pennsylvania, 1974.

Downs, Joseph. *Pennsylvania German Arts and Crafts: A Picture Book*. Metropolitan Museum of Art, New York, New York, 1949.

Egeland, Janice A. *Descendants of Christian Fisher and Other Amish Mennonite Pioneer Families*. Moore Clinic, Johns Hopkins Hospital, Baltimore, Maryland, 1972.

Estep, William. *The Anabaptist Story*. William B. Eerdmans Publishing Co., Grand Rapids, Michigan, revised edition, 1975.

Fabian, Monroe H. *Pennsylvania German Decorated Chest*. Main Street Press, New York, New York, 1978.

Fisher, Gideon L. *Farm Life and Its Changes*. Pequea Publishers, Gordonville, Pennsylvania, 1978.

Fisher, Sara E. and Stahl, Rachel K. *The Amish School*. Good Books, Intercourse, Pennsylvania, 1986.

Garvan, Beatrice B. *A Craftsman's Handbook, Henry Lapp*. Philadelphia Museum of Art, Philadelphia, Pennsylvania, 1975.

Garvan, Beatrice B. *The Pennsylvania German Collection*. Philadelphia Museum of Art, Philadelphia, Pennsylvania, 1982.

Gascho, Milton. "The Amish Division, 1693–1697, in Switzerland and Alsace," *Mennonite Quarterly Review*, XI (October, 1937), pp. 235–266.

Gehret, Ellen J. and Keyser, Alan. *The Homespun Textile Tradition of the Pennsylvania Germans*. Pennsylvania Historical and Museum Commission, Harrisburg, Pennsylvania, 1975.

Gehret, Ellen. *This is the Way I Pass My Time*. Pennsylvania German Society, Birdsboro, Pennsylvania, 1985.

Getz, Jane C. "The Economic Organization and Practices of the Old Order Amish of Lancaster County, Pennsylvania," *Mennonite Quarterly Review*, XX (January and April, 1946), pp. 53–80, 98–127.

Gingerich, Hugh F. and Kreider, Rachel W. *Amish and Amish Mennonite Genealogies*. Pequea Publishers, Gordonville, Pennsylvania, 1976.

Gingerich, Melvin. *Mennonite Attire through the Centuries*. Pennsylvania German Society, Birdsboro, Pennsylvania, 1970.

Glassie, Henry. "Folk Art," *Folklore and Folklife*. University of Chicago Press, Chicago, Illinois, 1972.

Glassie, Henry. *Passing the Time in Ballmemone*. University of Pennsylvania Press, Philadelphia, Pennsylvania, 1982.

Glassie, Henry. *Pattern in the Material Folk Culture of the Eastern United States*. University of Pennsylvania Press, Philadelphia, Pennsylvania, 1968.

Hartzler, H. Harold, *The King Family History*. Private publication, 1984.

Heaney, Howell J. and Weiser, Frederick S. *The Pennsylvania German Fraktur of the Free Library of Philadelphia*. Pennsylvania German Society, Breinigsville, Pennsylvania, 1976.

Holstein, Jonathan. *The Pieced Quilt*. McClelland and Stewart Ltd., Toronto, Ontario, 1973.

Hoover, Amos B. and Kanagy, Ezra J. *Two Old Letters by Hans Nafziger (1782)*. Published by Kanagy, Belleville, Pennsylvania, 1983.

Hostetler, John A. *Amish Society*. Johns Hopkins University Press, Baltimore, Maryland, 3rd edition, 1980.

Hostetler, John A. "Memoirs of Shem Zook (1798–1880), A Biography, "*Mennonite Quarterly Review*, 1964, pp. 280–299.

Hostetler, John A. "The Life and Times of Samuel Yoder (1824–1884)," *Mennonite Quarterly Review*, 1948, pp. 226–241.

Jenkins, J. Geraint. "The Use of Artifacts and Folk Art in the Folk Museum," *Folklore and Folklife*. University of Chicago Press, Chicago, Illinois, 1972.

Kallir, Jane. *The Folk Art Tradition*. Viking Press, New York, New York, 1982.

Kauffman, Henry J. *Pennsylvania Dutch American Folk Art*. Dover Publications, New York, New York, revised edition, 1964.

Kauffman, S. Duane. "Miscellaneous Amish Mennonite Documents," *Pennsylvania Mennonite Heritage*, July 1979, pp.

12–16.

Klamkin, Charles. *Weather Vanes, the History, Manufacture and Design of an American Folk Art*. Hawthorn Books, New York, New York, 1973.

Kopp, Joel and Kate. *American Hooked and Sewn Rugs*. E. P. Dutton, New York, New York, 1985.

Lestz, Gerald S. *Amish Culture and Economy*. Science Press, Ephrata, Pennsylvania, 1984.

Lichten, Francis M. *Folk Art of Rural Pennsylvania*. Bonanza Books, New York, New York, 1946.

Lipman, Ican and Winchester, Alice. *The Flowering of American Folkart (1776–1876)*. Viking Press, New York, New York, 1974.

Madigan, Mary Jean. *Americana Folk and Decorative Art*. Art and Antiques, New York, New York, 1982.

Mast, John B. *Letters of the Amish Division*. Christian Schlabach Publishing and Mennonite Publishing House, Scottdale, Pennsylvania, undated.

Miller, Harvey J. "Proceedings of Amish Ministers' Conferences, 1826–31," *Mennonite Quarterly Review*, XXXIII (1959), pp. 132–142.

Mittelberger, Gottlieb (trans. by O. Handin and J. Olive). "Journey to Pennsylvania," *The Diary*, January, 1979.

Old Order Map Committee. *Pennsylvania Amish Directory, Lancaster and Chester County Districts, 1973*. Pequea Publishers, Gordonville, Pennsylvania, 1973.

Pellman, Kenneth and Rachel. *Amish Crib Quilts*. Good Books, Intercourse, Pennsylvania, 1985.

Pellman, Kenneth and Rachel. *Amish Doll Quilts, Dolls, and Other Playthings*. Good Books, Intercourse, Pennsylvania, 1986.

Pellman, Kenneth and Rachel. *The World of Amish Quilts*. Good Books, Intercourse, Pennsylvania, 1984.

Schiffer, Margaret. *Miniature Antique Furniture*. Livingston Publishers, Wynnewood, Pennsylvania, 1972.

Scott, Stephen. *Why Do They Dress That Way?* Good Books, Intercourse, Pennsylvania, 1986.

Sebba, Anne. *Samplers*. Thames & Hudson, New York, New York, 1979.

Seitz, Ruth Hoover and Seitz, Blair. *Amish Country*. Crescent Books, New York, New York, 1987.

Silber, Julie. *Catalog of the Esprit Quilt Collection*. Esprit de Corp., San Francisco, California, 1985.

Smith, Elmer L. *The Amish Today: An Analysis of Their Beliefs, Behavior and Contemporary Problems*. The Proceedings of the Pennsylvania German Folklore Society, Vol. 24, Allentown, Pennsylvania, 1960.

Stoltzfus, Christine. *Golden Memories, Amos J. Stoltzfus*. Pequea Publishers, Gordonville, Pennsylvania, 1984.

Stoltzfus, Grant M. "History of the First Amish Mennonite Communities in America," *Mennonite Quarterly Review*, XVIII (1954), pp. 235–262.

Stoudt, John J. *Early Pennsylvania Arts & Crafts*. A.S. Barnes & Co., New York, New York, 1964.

Stoudt, John J. *Sunbonnets and Shoofly Pies*. Castle Books, New York, New York, 1973.

Swank, Scott T. *The Arts of the Pennsylvania Germans*. W. W. Norton Co., New York, New York, 1983.

Tortora, Vincent R. "The Courtship and Wedding Practices of the Old Order Amish," *Pennsylvania Folklore*, Spring, 1958.

Umble, John. "An Amish Minister's Manual," *Mennonite Quarterly Review*, XV (April, 1941), pp. 95–117.

Umble, John. "Amish Ordination Charges," *Mennonite Quarterly Review*, XIII (October, 1939), pp. 233–250.

Umble, John. "Amish Service Manuals," *Mennonite Quarterly Review*, XV (January, 1941), pp. 26–32.

Umble, John. "Catalog of an Amish Bishop's Library," *Mennonite Quarterly Review*, XX (July, 1946), pp. 230–239.

Umble, John. "Manuscript Amish Minister's Manuals in the Goshen College Mennonite Historical Library," *Mennonite Quarterly Review*, XV (October, 1941), pp. 243–251.

Umble, John. "Memoirs of an Amish Bishop," *Mennonite Quarterly Review*, XXII (April, 1948), pp. 94–115.

Umble, John. "The Old Order Amish of Lancaster County, Pennsylvania," extended book review, *Mennonite Quarterly Review*, XVII (October, 1943), pp. 207–236.

Warren, James A. and Denlinger, Donald M. *The Gentle People: A Portrait of the Amish*. Mill Bridge Museum, Soudersburg, Pennsylvania and Grossman Publishers, New York, 1969.

Weissman, Judith and Lavitt, Wendy. *Labors of Love: America's Textile and Needlework, 1650–1930*. Knopf, New York, New York, 1987.

Witmer, Margaret A. "Henry and Elizabeth Lapp, Amish Folk Artists," *Antique Collecting*, May 1979.

Yoder, Elmer S. *The Beachy Amish Mennonite Fellowship Churches*. Diakonia Ministries, Hartville, Ohio, 1987.

Yoder, Joseph W. *Rosanna of the Amish*. Herald Press, Scottdale, Pennsylvania, 1940.

Yoder, Paton. "Tennessee John Stoltzfus and the Great Schism in the Amish Church, 1850–77," *Pennsylvania Mennonite Heritage*, July, 1979, pp. 17–23.

Yoder, Paton. *Tennessee John Stoltzfus: Amish Church-Related Documents and Family Letters*. Lancaster Mennonite Historical Society, Lancaster, Pennsylvania, 1987.

Index

About the Authors

Kathryn and Dan McCauley married in 1968. They had a mutual interest in antiques and began to collect artifacts together shortly thereafter.

Their fascination with Amish decorative art began a decade ago when they saw and purchased their first quilt made by an Old Order craftsperson. As their interest grew, the McCauleys began to attend Amish farm sales and to become acquainted with members of the group in an effort to obtain the histories behind the objects they were collecting. They also began learning how the decorative products of the Amish reflect the people's culture and principles.

Dan graduated from St. Joseph's University with a major in Psychology and from the University of Pennsylvania with a major in Business. Kathryn also attended the University of Pennsylvania. For several years she operated a business in Philadelphia, selling contemporary Amish crafts and art.

Today the McCauleys live in Wynnewood, Pennsylvania, with their two children, Dan and Cayce.